-9 MAR 2019

22 APR 2023

Alan Titchmarsh
how to garden

Wildlife Gardening

BOOKS

10 9 8 7 6 5 4 3 2 1

Published in 2011 by BBC Books, an imprint of
Ebury Publishing, a Random House Group Company

The Random House Group Limited Reg. No. 954009

Addresses for companies within the Random House
Group can be found at www.randomhouse.co.uk

FSC
www.fsc.org
MIX
Paper from
responsible sources
FSC™ C004592

The Random House Group Limited
supports The Forest Stewardship
Council (FSC), the leading
international forest certification
organisation. All our titles that are
printed on Greenpeace approved
FSC certified paper carry the FSC
logo. Our paper procurement
policy can be found at www.
rbooks.co.uk/environment

A CIP catalogue record for this book is available from
the British Library.

ISBN 978 1 84 607409 7

Produced by OutHouse!
Shalbourne, Marlborough, Wiltshire SN8 3QJ

BBC BOOKS
COMMISSIONING EDITOR: Lorna Russell
PROJECT EDITOR: Caroline McArthur
PRODUCTION: David Brimble

OUTHOUSE!
COMMISSIONING EDITOR: Sue Gordon
SERIES EDITOR: Polly Boyd
SERIES ART EDITOR: Robin Whitecross
CONTRIBUTING EDITOR: Julia Cady
EDITOR: Anna Kruger
DESIGNER: Louise Turpin
ILLUSTRATIONS by Julia Cady, Lizzie Harper, Janet Tanner
PHOTOGRAPHS by Jonathan Buckley except where
credited otherwise on page 128
CONCEPT DEVELOPMENT & SERIES DESIGN:
Elizabeth Mallard-Shaw, Sharon Cluett

Colour origination by Altaimage, London
Printed and bound by Firmengruppe APPL,
Wemding, Germany

Contents

Introduction

Gardening is one of the best and most fulfilling activities on earth, but it can sometimes seem complicated and confusing. The answers to problems can usually be found in books, but big fat gardening books can be rather daunting. Where do you start? How can you find just the information you want without wading through lots of stuff that is not appropriate to your particular problem? Well, a good index is helpful, but sometimes a smaller book devoted to one particular subject fits the bill better – especially if it is reasonably priced and if you have a small garden where you might not be able to fit in everything suggested in a larger volume.

The *How to Garden* books aim to fill that gap – even if sometimes it may be only a small one. They are clearly set out and written, I hope, in a straightforward, easy-to-understand style. I don't see any point in making gardening complicated, when much of it is based on common sense and observation. (All the key techniques are explained and illustrated, and I've included plenty of tips and tricks of the trade.)

There are suggestions on the best plants and the best varieties to grow in particular situations and for a particular effect. I've tried to keep the information crisp and to the point so that you can find what you need quickly and easily and then put your new-found knowledge into practice. Don't worry if you're not familiar with the Latin names of plants. They are there to make sure you can find the plant as it will be labelled in the nursery or garden centre, but where appropriate I have included common names, too. Forgetting a plant's name need not stand in your way when it comes to being able to grow it.

Above all, the *How to Garden* books are designed to fill you with passion and enthusiasm for your garden and all that its creation and care entails, from designing and planting it to maintaining it and enjoying it. For more than fifty years gardening has been my passion, and that initial enthusiasm for watching plants grow, for trying something new and for just being outside pottering has never faded. If anything I am keener on gardening now than I ever was and get more satisfaction from my plants every day. It's not that I am simply a romantic, but rather that I have learned to look for the good in gardens and in plants, and there is lots to be found. Oh, there are times when I fail – when my plants don't grow as well as they should and I need to try harder. But where would I rather be on a sunny day? Nowhere!

The *How to Garden* handbooks will, I hope, allow some of that enthusiasm – childish though it may be – to rub off on you, and the information they contain will, I hope, make you a better gardener, as well as opening your eyes to the magic of plants and flowers.

Introducing wildlife gardening

With their wide range of plants to provide food and shelter for wildlife, gardens have become an increasingly important refuge for insects, birds and animals as more and more wild habitats disappear. Our gardens can offer fantastic opportunities to get close to the natural world, and many creatures can readily be persuaded to take up residence in them. A wildlife garden is rewarding, and easy to get going, and can be just as thrilling for some as an exotic holiday (not to mention kinder to the environment and your bank balance). And it's right outside your door, for 365 days of the year.

What is wildlife gardening?

Practically all gardens attract some kind of wildlife, and most gardeners wouldn't want it any other way. The activities of blackbirds, blue tits and insects such as butterflies and bees really bring a garden to life. There are, admittedly, a few drawbacks such as caterpillar-nibbled plants and stolen fruit, but most of us are happy to put up with these in exchange for the rich environment that a garden alive with wild creatures offers.

With luck, your wildlife gardening efforts will mean that seeing birds feeding young, like this robin, becomes a regular occurrence – but it never, ever loses its magic.

Changing times

Until the mid-20th century, the whole idea of wildlife gardening might have seemed puzzling. The countryside was where wildlife belonged, conservation was scarcely necessary and gardens were no place for most wild creatures. It was just taken for granted that gardeners would wipe out, by fair means or foul, any 'pests' that interfered with their crops, without much thought for any unintended consequences.

Since the 1940s, changing farming practices and increasing development have left fewer and fewer toeholds for rural wildlife. A huge percentage of the best wildlife habitats has been lost for ever to roads, buildings, car parks and vast, featureless areas of chemically managed agriculture. Birds and animals that were very familiar only a generation ago, including hedgehogs, house sparrows, song thrushes and cuckoos, are now in serious decline. Fortunately, the value of wild habitats is now recognized and gardeners' attitudes to wildlife are changing.

Gardens to the rescue

With their diversity of plants, their ponds, hedges, flower borders and undisturbed nooks and crannies, gardens add up to a vast area of wildlife-friendly land, in both the town and the country. They have rather unexpectedly stepped into the breach as a refuge for some of the wild creatures that are being squeezed out by pesticides and habitat loss.

More and more gardeners are also discovering what a privilege it is to be a self-appointed wildlife warden. Driven by the wish to offer help, or simply by the joy of watching and getting to know the creatures that share our gardens, we are learning to adapt our gardening habits to accommodate them, and finding that they respond to the slightest encouragement. So why wait?

Ten steps towards a wildlife garden

- Stop using chemical pesticides and weedkillers; these may harm wildlife.
- Replace a section of fencing with a mixed native hedge (see pages 32–3).
- Make a compost heap (see pages 54–5).
- Plant at least one tree (see pages 58–9).
- Increase numbers of bee and butterfly plants like *Eryngium*, shown right (see also pages 70–1).
- Plant some winter-flowering nectar plants (see page 123).
- Let a small area of grass grow longer.
- Leave some fallen leaves to rot down naturally.
- Build a log pile.
- Delay cutting down most of your perennial plants until spring.

Welcoming wildlife: the basics

Whether gardeners or not, many people enjoy a touch of nature in the garden. Feeding birds has become hugely popular, and may help explain increases in the populations of great tits, goldfinches and great spotted woodpeckers. Garden ponds are important habitats for frogs and other amphibians, and it's exciting when spawn arrives in the spring. A visiting or resident hedgehog is a delight, while a summer garden seems incomplete without its butterflies and bees.

The garden's support system

Wildlife-watching can be very absorbing while we're in the garden, or when looking out of the window as we stand at the kitchen sink or talk on the phone. But the vital support network that sustains a good wildlife garden is something that we may not be very aware of. Indeed, we may not be able to see it at all – at least, not without a strong hand-lens or even a microscope. A healthy garden wildlife population relies on a whole complex web of interdependent relationships between plants and the many creatures – tiny or large – that depend upon them and upon each other. It's a continuous daily drama in which the roles of soil bacteria, mites, fungi and aphids are just as

A large garden (here, Beth Chatto's in Essex) may have many wonderful plants from around the world, but there's a place for native wildflowers too.

Multi-tasking features in the garden

Plants and water features that fulfil more than one role at a time – or better still, at more than one time – are a wildlife gardener's best friends. They really do earn their space, especially in a small garden. Teasels and thistles, for example, supply both summer nectar for butterflies and bees, and winter seeds for birds. Cotoneasters and mature ivy plants offer nectar, berries and perhaps a place to nest; a crab apple tree has all these and may also attract aphids for blue tits to feed on. Eventually its topmost branches might serve as a perch for a blackbird or greenfinch to sing from. A pond is definitely among the best multi-purpose wildlife facilities. Not just a potential breeding habitat for amphibians, dragonflies and many insects, it also functions as a drinking place for birds and mammals, as well as a home for plants of water and wetland.

Don't forget

Dead vegetation is just as important for many insects and other invertebrates as living plants. Leave piles of dead wood in the garden for beetles, woodlice and centipedes to feed and shelter in. Like all plant matter, it will eventually rot away as part of nature's ingenious recycling scheme, sustaining fungi and other plants in the process.

Friends or foes?

Open your arms and your garden to wildlife and you become a potential host for many delightful creatures. It's not their fault if some of them – from foxes and rabbits to pigeons and mice – see your garden as an opportunity to eat things you'd prefer they didn't, or to raise their families in an inconvenient place. Like a lot of things that are worth doing, wildlife gardening isn't straightforward, and you will often have to make difficult decisions in steering the tricky course between the needs of wildlife and your own. Only you can decide where to draw the line, but before you resort to desperate measures to get rid of them, it's a good idea to try one of the many simple and harmless deterrents (*see* pages 50–3). These aren't foolproof but they may be all that's necessary to persuade the miscreants to go somewhere else instead.

important as those of woodpeckers, frogs and hedgehogs. Each member of the cast supports others, and each depends in turn on others somewhere else in the web. The best kind of wildlife gardening involves creating the right conditions for this multi-layered support network, while disturbing it as little as possible.

The place of plants

Plants form the basis of the garden's ability to support and sustain wild creatures, and, in short, the more the merrier. Without plants there would be no wildlife. Gardens have a unique status here, with a variety of plants large and small, from trees to grasses, that may have their origins pretty well anywhere in the world. If you think you don't have many plants in your garden, try counting the different kinds of shrubs and border plants, not forgetting the apple tree, the herbs perhaps ... and that ivy on the fence. Remember to include the weeds, too! You may be very surprised at the total. And somewhere out there are various creatures – from caterpillars and bugs to birds and mammals – that find a use for most of them.

Most gardens can accommodate a few wildflowers such as foxgloves and ox-eye daisies. Different flower shapes attract different nectar-seeking insects, so aim for variety.

Go native

A proportion of plant-eating insects, such as moth caterpillars, will eat a surprisingly wide range of plants and appear not to mind whether they are native or not. But it's a good idea to plant at least some natives in your wildlife garden because certain insect species are a little pickier. Native trees, in particular, tend to support a wider range of insects than most of the more exotic non-natives, so try to include one, at least (see pages 58–9).

Natural pest control

In an ideal world herbivores would eat only weeds and predators would eat only pests. Of course, life isn't quite like that, but in some cases things do work to the gardener's advantage. Aphids, such as greenfly and blackfly, make a nuisance of themselves by sucking sap from your plants, but they are eaten in large numbers by many other creatures, from blue tits and wrens to hoverfly larvae and ladybirds. Caterpillars, plump from nibbling your Brussels sprouts and peas, are taken by many parent birds for their young, or are parasitized by certain wasps. Song thrushes are well known for finding snails particularly appetizing, and hedgehogs eat slugs.

These natural pest-control processes can be tremendously beneficial in the garden, but wildlife gardening entails creating and managing a whole habitat, while trying to maintain a natural balance, rather than targeting individual creatures. However, the richer your habitat becomes, the less likely you are to have overwhelming pest problems as each species finds its place in the complex web where one creature lives off another.

Problems with pesticides

It is when we disrupt the garden's web that trouble can start. Some chemical controls, for example, have caused serious damage. The most notorious, DDT, was used widely, from the 1940s to the 1970s, as an insecticide by farmers and gardeners. Its persistence allowed it to make its way up the food chain in increasing concentrations, and it began to accumulate permanently in the bodies of larger predators such as birds of prey. Some could no longer breed successfully because the effect of the chemical was to make their eggs too thin-shelled to be viable. The DDT used in those decades is detectable in our oceans even today. Fortunately, its use – and that of many other persistent pesticides – has long since been banned, but the principle still stands: sometimes the unwanted effects of chemical controls aren't understood until it's too late. It seems no coincidence that more garden chemicals every year are being withdrawn from sale on safety grounds, and all of us may have to get used to alternatives eventually.

Another reason for laying off the pesticides is that they are nearly all non-specific, so they can kill useful predators as well as the pests. Pest populations recover quickly because pests tend to be resilient (which is why they're considered pests), and

When you watch a song thrush dispatching a snail the natural way it may make you hesitate to use chemical slug and snail killers.

Giving up pesticides

If you have been a regular pesticide user but have resolved to chuck away the chemicals, then you can expect the first season or two to test your nerve. It takes a while for a balanced ecosystem to evolve, and there will probably be the occasional boom in slug or aphid numbers along the way. It's easy to panic unnecessarily about garden pests and diseases, though. Deterrents and natural pest control methods will help (*see* pages 51–3), and healthy plants will often shrug off problems by themselves. Whatever happens, stick with it and try not to reach for the spray in a weak moment. It's a good feeling to know exactly what has gone into your apples and lettuces, and you and your garden wildlife will probably never look back.

Don't forget

Once you have made the decision to go pesticide-free, make sure you dispose safely of any garden chemicals remaining in your shed or garage. Most local authorities offer special facilities where you can take such hazardous waste, and should be able to advise you.

Lavender, fennel, mullein and poppies are all star wildlife plants. Here, they form part of a relaxed, colourful tumble of flowers that would be a real pleasure to sit or walk among – or to fly among, if you're a butterfly or a bee!

damaging the predator populations just encourages the pests to stay one step ahead.

Laid-back gardening

Not using pesticides is just one key example of the principle of 'live and let live' – such an important part of wildlife gardening and an attitude worth cultivating. Try to develop a more relaxed approach to the garden (*see* pages 18–19) and be a little less tidy. Many creatures are easily disturbed from hiding places

by over-zealous trimming and sweeping: frequently, the only encouragement they need to settle in with you is to be left alone. Respect the wildlife you have invited into your garden, and encourage others to do the same. Get into the habit of watching quietly and unobtrusively, without making sudden movements or noises, and

the birds and animals will get used to you, becoming tamer and more trusting. Your garden will feel like a calmer, more soothing place – one that is more attractive to wildlife and therapeutic for people, too. Indeed, the benefits of a few minutes' quiet nature watching at the beginning or at the end of a hectic day are very apparent to anyone who has done it.

Wildlife-friendly design

Design and wildlife are sometimes assumed to be at opposite ends of the gardening spectrum. They certainly needn't be, but planning a garden that is as close as possible to ideal for you and your wildlife does takes a bit of thought. A well-designed space that is practical and enjoyable to use, easy on the eye, but also appealing to the birds and bees is perfectly achievable, and it's worth getting it right. A little planning and forethought mean you will not only do a better job for wildlife, but you'll end up with a garden that meets your own needs, too.

Designing a wildlife garden isn't so very different from designing any other kind of garden. It's largely a practical matter of making the best use of the space for what you want your particular garden to do and be. It's about creating variety and interest. It's also about solving problems, from a damp patch to a grim view, or how to make a small space appear bigger. And, of course, it's about making the garden look as attractive and inviting as you possibly can.

What kind of garden?

The first thing to ask yourself when you begin to plan is how committed you want to be. Is your ideal more wildlife than garden, or more garden than wildlife? Are you more a wildlife warden than a gardener, content to let nature take over your garden and intervening only to improve it as a

In a successful wildlife garden, thoughtful planting design should not be very far away – but it need never be obvious. This flower border feels relaxed and informal and is a magnet for insects, but shape, texture and rhythm have all been considered.

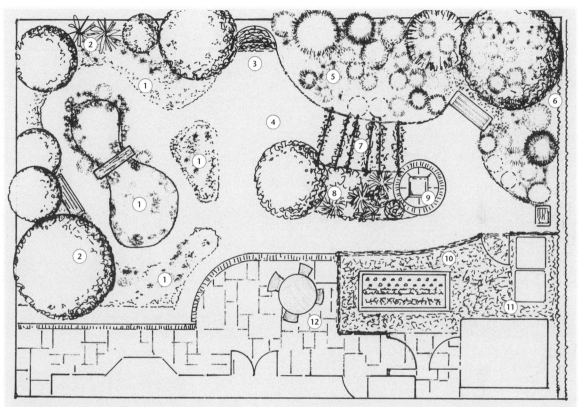

1 Pond and long grass with wildflowers (*see* page 39 for planting detail)
2 Woodland-edge area with spring woodland flowers
3 Woven-willow arbour
4 Paths and clearings with mown grass
5 Nectar border (*see* page 71 for planting detail)
6 Mixed native hedge (*see* page 33)
7 Three double timber arches planted with climbers
8 Border planted for autumn colour, and winter seeds and berries
9 Bird table on paved circle
10 Kitchen garden with 90cm (3ft) fence of woven willow and a raised vegetable bed
11 Shed and compost area; surface of chipped bark or gravel
12 Paved patio with table and chairs

A VARIED WILDLIFE GARDEN FOR ALL-YEAR INTEREST
10 x 15M (33 x 50FT)

About a third of the garden is a wild area with a pond, wildflowers in longer grass, and native trees and shrubs. Flower and shrub borders have a wide variety of plants to please insects, birds and gardeners alike. Mown paths create glades and views, and the enclosed kitchen garden includes a shed and compost area.

wildlife habitat – treating it, in other words, as a small-scale nature reserve? Or are you first and foremost a keen gardener, but willing to allow nature into your plot as long as it doesn't make it too untidy or threaten your vegetables and roses? Most of us stand somewhere in between. Getting the balance right, for both you and your wildlife, is a key part of developing a good design.

Existing features

When you begin creating a wildlife garden, you won't normally be having to start from scratch. There are few gardens that contain no wildlife at all, and unless you have a brand-new plot you will usually be able to build on what's already there and include at least some existing features in your design. It may be possible – and will be less expensive and disruptive – to renovate and

A well-positioned seat, with satisfying views both to and from it, can be a key feature. If you get it right, it will be a real pleasure to use.

reuse existing hard landscaping such as paving or a pergola. A tough border perennial that is obviously happy in your plot may be worth splitting up to include in a new planting scheme, or there may be a gaunt old shrub that shelters ladybirds in its cracks and crevices in winter, and provides summer nectar for butterflies and bees. Even if it's no longer a thing of beauty, keep it for the time being and replace or hard prune it only when you have created some alternative locations for its inhabitants.

Start by taking a hard, critical look at your plot, and perhaps by roughly sketching an outline plan. Plot the boundaries, the house with its doors and windows, and existing features that are difficult or impossible to move, or that you may want to keep: access gates, inspection covers, an oil tank, paving and steps, a shed or greenhouse perhaps, trees and certain other plants, hedges, and so on. This is the time to record views out of the garden, noting which you would like to keep and where you need screening. Also, notice the limiting characteristics of particular parts of the garden: climatic factors such as sun, shade and windy areas;

Don't forget

Height! The all-important third dimension is easy to overlook when planning a garden. The positioning of trees and of structures such as arches and pergolas, which create height instantly, can make or break a design.

Continuity in the border

One of the most important aspects of any planting design is to keep a garden interesting throughout the year, with no dull interludes when there is little to look at. The majority of wildflowers bloom for a relatively short period, but there are many border plants (listed below) that both have a long season of interest and are also attractive to many forms of wildlife, so try and include some of these plants and your garden won't have an 'off' season.

Acanthus

Allium cristophii

Anthemis tinctoria 'E.C. Buxton'

Aster × frikartii 'Mönch'

Diascia

Echinacea purpurea

Erigeron karvinskianus

Euphorbia polychroma

Geranium 'Ann Folkard'

Geranium 'Rozanne'

Geranium sanguineum

Penstemon 'Andenken an Friedrich Hahn'

Persicaria amplexicaulis 'Firetail'

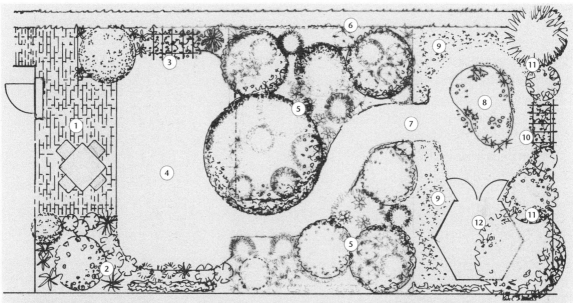

1 Brick-paved terrace with table and chairs
2 Flower border with shrubs and wall shrubs for screening
3 Timber pergola planted with climbers; seat beneath
4 Lawn
5 Woodland area (*see* page 65 for planting detail)
6 Mixed native hedge
7 Mown path through woodland and around pond
8 Pond
9 Flowering lawn
10 Timber pergola (as **3**)
11 Shrubs and tree for screening
12 Summerhouse

A COTTAGE-STYLE GARDEN WITH SECLUDED POND
15 x 7.5M (50 x 25FT)

Although not large, this garden is divided into three quite different areas. Near the house is a small brick terrace with flower borders and a lawn. From here a grass path leads through a woodland area with a 'wilder' feel to a wildlife pond with a summerhouse. Two climber-clad pergolas make focal points, with seats beneath them for wildlife-watching.

changes of level; damp and dry areas and points where underground services may run. Record all these features carefully: you'll need to work round them when planning your layout and again when choosing the plants.

The second part of the planning process is to make a wish list of features you would like to have in the garden: a seating area or two, overhead screening or shade, a place to dry the washing, a compost heap, a pond and bird-feeding station, a mini-woodland or meadow, a butterfly border and so on. Plan the garden not only to attract wildlife, but also to maximize opportunities for watching the birds and animals that may arrive – both in the garden and from the house. Include at least a couple of places to sit, perhaps at different times of day. A well-chosen seat or arbour is not just a practical addition, it also makes an effective focal point at the end of a view.

Consider every little corner for its wildlife potential. Here, water, a pebble beach and a sculptural tree-stump add up to a really rich habitat.

Rethinking your garden for wildlife

Turning your garden into a better place for wildlife is just about the easiest adaptation you could make, involving next to no trouble or expense. What you may need to do, though, is to question the reasons why you garden in the way that you do, and imagine how it would be if you made some changes. Conventional gardening embraces many practices from a bygone age. Some still make perfect sense, but for others the writing is on the wall and it's time to change.

The tidy gardener

For some people, gardening is just another chore, perhaps with little pleasure attached. Often, the people who look at it this way tend to want their gardens to be just as neat and clean as their houses, with everything mown, swept and weeded and not a leaf out of place. Would-be wildlife gardeners will need to ease themselves gradually out of the parade-ground approach to gardening. And the upside?

There's a strong possibility that you'll start to find your garden a whole lot more interesting as well as enjoying it more.

Lawns

A bowling-green lawn can look great as part of a garden design, setting off planting perfectly. But if you're not obsessive about your lawn, you can easily let go of the notion that the whole thing has to be mown within an inch of its life every week, and sprayed regularly to keep it free from weeds and moss. Mowing less frequently will often mean healthier grass that shades out the competition better. Try letting a small, clearly defined area grow into a flowering lawn (*see* pages 40–1). Insects and birds are sure to like it, and perhaps you will too.

What is a weed?

Many of us have been unwittingly conditioned to see weeds as one of the chief evils of the garden, but it's worth stopping to think where you stand in relation to your weeds. Nobody wants to see their beans or strawberries smothered by nettles and docks, and you won't find many devotees of bindweed or ground elder. But not everything that arrives in your garden uninvited is to be sent packing. Being a bit more relaxed about weeds can lead to some pleasant surprises and worthwhile discoveries.

Different gardeners' tolerance of weeds will vary, and you must decide what you can put up with. Many gardeners wouldn't entertain rosebay willowherb, for instance, which can be rather rampant if you don't cut it down before it sets seed. (The white form, *Chamerion angustifolium* 'Album', is better behaved.) But if you look among its lower leaves in summer you may find the remarkable caterpillars of the

Longer grass studded with flowers can look really attractive, and daisies, dandelions and clover will be much appreciated by insects and birds. So try not to see all 'weeds' as enemies.

Columbines and ox-eye daisies are the easiest of plants – ideal for a relaxed, 'cottagey' look. Ace self-seeders, they pop up in places where you may never have thought to plant them.

exquisite elephant hawkmoth, complete with 'eyes' and a 'trunk'. Such discoveries may make you view at least some of your weeds in a different light.

Know your seedlings

It's well worth getting to know the commoner garden weeds at the seedling stage. If you recognize one as a potential troublemaker, you can tweak it out in a second, whereas if you leave it to grow and put down roots you may have a major digging job on your hands. Many wildflowers and garden plants (*see* pages 30–1) will self-sow just as enthusiastically as weeds, and are frequently treated as such. But again, learn to recognize as many as you can at an early stage and perhaps learn to leave alone those you can't. Wholesale hoeing in the interests of neatness can rob both you and your insect population of a host of interesting flowers. Self-sowers also have a habit of putting themselves in just the right place, where they often make excellent, healthy plants – so don't

spurn these free gifts just because you haven't planted them yourself.

Autumn leaves

The advent of leaf blowers has tended to make gardeners keener than ever to clear up fallen leaves. It's best not to let them lie in damp drifts on the lawn, where they keep light and air from reaching the grass.

When blown into borders and under hedges, on the other hand, leaves can be left as an insulating blanket that will protect the soil from winter weather and may even provide useful bedding for a hibernating hedgehog. Eventually, soil organisms will help the dead leaves break down into soil-conditioning humus, completing nature's woodland cycle.

Don't forget

Formal hedging such as yew and box looks undeniably smart when kept crisply clipped, but not all hedges have to be so tightly controlled. Hedging plants such as hawthorn, blackthorn and dog rose will flower and fruit more abundantly under a relaxed trimming regime, and will be better for wildlife.

Green manure

Fallow land will generally be in better heart if it's kept covered with greenery. You can plant seeds of so-called 'green manures', such as grazing rye, winter tares and phacelia, but young annual weed plants do the job almost as well, and you don't have to bother to sow them. Don't leave them long enough to set seed, though. In many parts of the garden you can simply dig them in, a couple of weeks before you want to plant the area. They will add humus and minerals to the soil.

Autumn leaves provide a free and effortless winter mulch, so don't be obsessive about clearing them up when they blow into your borders.

An environmentally sustainable garden goes hand-in-hand with wildlife gardening: people who care for their garden wildlife tend to be concerned for the wider environment, too. More and more of us are trying to make our gardens greener in all sorts of ways, from saving water and recycling to avoiding chemical controls or peat-based compost.

Choosing and re-using materials

There are many changes you can make, small- as well as large-scale, to reduce your carbon footprint as a gardener. Here are a few ideas to get you started:

■ Use natural materials wherever you can. Consider using recycled bricks or paving slabs instead of new ones for hard landscaping projects, and re-use materials within the garden as much as possible. If you have to buy new timber, make sure it is responsibly sourced – look for the Forest Stewardship Council (FSC) logo.

■ Try to buy locally. Support local plant nurseries and perhaps find a source of locally produced charcoal for your barbecue. Consider where each item you purchase has come from.

■ Make sure any compost you buy is peat-free. Peat bogs are precious both as wildlife habitats and as a vast,

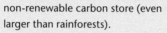

non-renewable carbon store (even larger than rainforests).

■ Choose clay or coir pots, which are biodegradable, and re-use any plastic pots and plant trays rather than just putting them in the bin.

■ Use solar-powered lights in the garden if you can. If you have mains lighting, use dim, low-energy bulbs. Switch lights off when not in use to save energy and avoid light pollution.

Consider using recycled building materials for new garden features.
① Old bricks make attractive paths (but may not resist frost for long).
② Recycled, untreated timbers like these are a popular way to edge raised beds.

Green gardening methods

Most of us are already taking a greener approach to our day-to-day gardening. Important changes to consider making (if you haven't already) include:

■ Get a good composting system going, and use it to recycle all your compostable household and garden waste (*see* pages 54–5).

■ Try to avoid any inorganic chemicals such as weedkillers, insecticides, fungicides and artificial fertilizers. Their manufacture uses a lot of energy, and they can leach into watercourses.

Make a tunnel, arbour or arch from living willow – it's sustainable, fast-growing and fun. Buy willow cuttings from a specialist nursery in winter (look online for suppliers and advice) and plant. Weave and tie the stems in as they grow, to form your chosen structure. Prune regularly to keep the shape.

■ Think of ways to reduce your dependency on power tools such as the strimmer, hedge trimmer, leaf blower and motor mower. Use hand tools whenever you can.

Managing water

With climate change, conserving water is becoming a major issue for gardeners. Temperate regions tend to get enough rain overall, but uneven distribution over the year increasingly results in flooding or droughts.

Urban areas are especially prone to flash flooding when heavy rain pours off hard surfaces into storm drains, soon overloading them. One solution is to install porous surfaces, such as gravel or permeable block paving, instead of tarmac, concrete or mortared paving slabs. Planning laws now apply to the surfacing of front gardens, so always check what's allowed in your area. Other landscaping measures to help with water management include rain gardens (*see* right) and green roofs (*see* page 49). Both slow down the progress of rainwater into drains and rivers, and both are good for wildlife.

Harvesting rainwater from roofs for use in the garden nearly always makes sense: it can be stored simply in a water butt or, on a larger scale, in an underground tank with appropriate pipework. More sophisticated water-recycling systems include ones for treating water from baths, showers and washing in the house. This 'grey

Think about where your rainwater goes next.

① A porous surface material such as shingle enables excess water to drain away slowly and naturally without the rapid runoff that can cause flooding.

② Channel as much rainwater as you can from roofs, storing it in containers, like this attractive wooden barrel.

water' should not be used untreated because of possible contamination by bacteria and detergents.

Of course, the simplest and cheapest way to conserve water is to manage with less. Here are some ideas:

■ Choose plants that don't need much water, if your soil is dry (*see* page 109).

■ Mulch flower borders in spring.

■ Grow vegetables more intensively in well-composted raised beds.

■ Water plants in the evening to reduce evaporation.

■ Target water around the roots of plants using a watering can rather than a sprinkler.

■ Plant trees and shrubs in autumn so they benefit from winter rain.

Don't forget

To prevent flash flooding, recent planning legislation has prohibited the laying of impermeable surfaces in front gardens without permission from your local authority.

Rain gardens

A versatile landscaping solution to the problem of too much or too little water, which is quickly catching on in both public and private spaces, is the rain garden. Here, rainwater from roofs and other impermeable surfaces is channelled by pipework and gullies into a specially constructed depression that becomes a temporary shallow pond. This is designed as an attractive garden feature with suitable planting that can tolerate short-term flooding. The plants take up some of the water, and permeable layers beneath filter the water and slow down its progress into streams and rivers, effectively reducing the risk of flooding. And the rain garden's mix of water and planting makes it a great refuge for wildlife. Suitable plants include dogwoods (*Cornus*), guelder rose (*Viburnum opulus*), coneflowers (*Rudbeckia* and *Echinacea*), Michaelmas daisies (*Aster novi-belgii*), *Eupatorium*, loosestrifes (*Lythrum* and *Lysimachia*) and *Iris sibirica*.

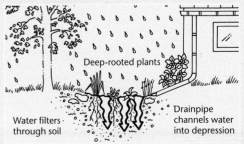

Deep-rooted plants

Water filters through soil

Drainpipe channels water into depression

Making a wildlife garden

The first step towards becoming a wildlife gardener is in some ways the easiest: it's about cultivating a relaxed attitude and learning to live and let live in the garden, giving wild creatures the chance to move in if they choose to. But, rather like the owner of a hotel or restaurant, there is quite a lot you can do to entice guests to come in, rather than just waiting for them to arrive.

Creating habitats

Gardens have a lot going for them as wildlife habitats. A typical street's worth of gardens is likely to contain a wide variety of plants, offering ideal food and shelter to many different forms of animal life from blackbirds to ladybirds. It has been estimated that gardens make up more than one-tenth of the land area of Britain, so your own garden is without doubt a great place to make a real difference to wildlife.

The male orange tip is a familiar butterfly. It emerges from a chrysalis in spring. Females may lay their eggs on cuckoo flower (here) or honesty.

Adapting your garden

Putting out food for the birds is how most people begin their relationship with garden wildlife, but creating a whole environment where your visitors will feel at home takes that relationship – as well as your chances of success as a wildlife gardener – several steps further. The wild habitat that gardens tend to resemble is what's known as 'woodland edge'. Fortunately for wildlife gardening, this is a very rich habitat because it is so varied, providing the right conditions for a whole range of sun- and shade-loving fauna and flora with its mix of trees, shrubs, grasses and flowers. A garden that offers something similar will be an excellent starting point for developing a more varied wildlife garden with several distinct habitats to attract the creatures whose tastes are more specialized.

Long grass, a lawn, trees and shrubs: this mix of habitats has the makings of a very successful wildlife garden, meeting the needs of all sorts of insects, birds and other creatures.

You may not be able to re-create a true bluebell wood, but many gardens offer plenty of scope for woodland-style planting and the effect can be wonderful.

few trees underplanted with a mixture of woodland flowers and you will soon enjoy the benefit of a wonderfully uplifting sight on a sunny spring day.

Which trees?

Choose your trees with care. Many of our much-loved native trees, such as oak and beech, will in time grow far larger than you imagine and may cause problems for you or your successors. They cast dense shade, and by the time they have outgrown their space there won't be much you can do without incurring correspondingly huge bills from a tree surgeon. But many much more manageable trees are good for wildlife, too (*see* pages 58–9). The right trees for your garden will depend largely on your soil and conditions, so notice which ones look right and do well in nearby gardens, parks and hedgerows. Native species, such as hazel, rowan, field maple and birch, have the edge as far as wildlife goes, so do try to include at least some of these 'wildings'. Small plants sold just for hedging can be bought very cheaply and will establish faster than large specimens. An alien tree or two among them will usually do no harm at all, and may even provide something the natives lack, such as juicy fruit at a particular season.

Planting and underplanting

As you plan your mini-woodland, consider the impact it may have on its surroundings. What will the trees shade as they grow taller, and how much will it matter? Can they be sited so they provide useful shelter?

Wildlife corridors

One of the problems associated with habitat destruction in the wild is that populations of the creatures living in those habitats can become isolated. For example, if the middle part of a long strip of forest is felled to build a road, some of the animals living in the remaining tree cover at either end no longer have access to each other. Their populations may become too small to be viable, and the genetic diversity that results when breeding takes place among a large population is lost. The same thing can apply to garden wildlife. If your garden is efficiently enclosed by fences and walls, then your frogs or hedgehogs won't be able to come into contact with those next door and their chances of successful breeding are reduced. Hedges between gardens make great 'wildlife corridors', providing safe travelling for small mammals and birds, reptiles and amphibians, and also for the many insects and mini-beasts that either don't fly, or are weak flyers. Gardens as wildlife habitats work best as parts of a whole, so make sure that your garden wildlife can get around and socialize.

Woodland

A bluebell wood in spring is surely one of the most thrilling highlights of the countryside year, and the kind of deciduous woodland carpeted with a range of wildflowers that our grandparents took for granted is a very rich wildlife habitat. Sadly, it is now a rarity outside nature reserves. Yet woodland has a very long ancestry and its legacy is huge numbers of wild species that are adapted to woodland living, from fungi and flowers to birds and beetles. Even if your garden is enormous, you can never replicate native woodland with all its complex webs of inhabitants, but some of these woodlanders may well decide to move in if you give them the conditions they like. Start with just a

Ground preparation should concentrate on incorporating moisture-retaining humus to get your trees and flowers safely through their first season or two without constant watering, and on getting rid of perennial weeds, which would soon dominate your carefully planted ground flora and turn it into a messy tangle.

Plant your chosen trees about 3–4m (10–13ft) apart. They will look very widely spaced to begin with, but plant them much closer and they will be overcrowded later. The choice for underplanting is very wide. A mixture of spring-flowering perennials and bulbs works well, and you may want to include some shrubs: native ones such as holly, butcher's broom, buckthorn, guelder rose (*Viburnum opulus*) and spurge laurel (*Daphne laureola*), and perhaps a couple of fragrant garden favourites such as wintersweet (*Sarcococca*) and *Mahonia* to give interest in winter. And don't forget climbers: ivy, honeysuckle and

In a layered planting scheme of trees, shrubs and perennials (here birches, viburnum and comfrey), the choice of alternatives for different effects over a long season is huge.

species clematis are all valued by wildlife for their nectar and berries or seeds. Woodland planting can look tatty after the end of spring, but you can brighten things up for summer by planting foxgloves, Welsh poppies and the more shade-tolerant campanulas and hardy geraniums.

Managing woodland

Historically, woodland was a valuable resource to be managed for its timber, and regular cutting meant that the tree cover did not become too dense for plants to grow beneath. One of the classic woodland practices was (and still is, in some areas) coppicing, where certain trees are cut and allowed to regenerate (*see* right). This sustainable practice creates ideal conditions for woodland wildflowers and makes garden-scale woodland very manageable.

Woodland wildflowers

Wood anemone (*Anemone nemorosa*)
Wood spurge (*Euphorbia amygdaloides*)
Sweet woodruff (*Galium odoratum*)
Stinking hellebore (*Helleborus foetidus*)
English bluebell (*Hyacinthoides non-scripta*)
Solomon's seal (*Polygonatum × hybridum*)
Primrose (*Primula vulgaris*)
Dog violet (*Viola riviniana*)

Don't forget

Keep the ground well weeded in the early stages of establishing woodland planting. It will take a while for the tree canopy to spread enough to begin to shade out undesirable vigorous grasses and weeds.

Coppicing trees

You don't need a huge garden to create a small area of coppice, and you'll be making your very own version of one of the richest woodland wildlife habitats. Hazel or, on damper ground, willow or alder are among suitable trees to use. Position young plants about 2–3m (6–10ft) apart and once they are established, cut them almost to the ground in winter, every four or five years. New stems will spring up within a few months. The trees never become unmanageable, and the process can be repeated indefinitely. Use the cut timber for pea-sticks, bean-poles, fencing and other garden structures, and to make log piles for wildlife: you'll soon think of plenty of uses for your own free wood supply. The ground around and underneath the coppice stubs is perfect for spring flowers: primroses, violets, bluebells and other woodland plants that make the most of the spring sunshine by flowering before the trees come into leaf.

Wetland

It's unlikely that you would want to turn your garden into a full-scale wetland habitat, and that could, anyway, be rather impractical. Introducing some water into your garden in the form of a pond or even just a boggy area, on the other hand, is easily done and is one of the best ways to make a difference to garden wildlife. Finding drinking water can be a real challenge for birds, especially in summer droughts or winter freezes. All kinds of other creatures, from hedgehogs to bees or dragonflies, are likely to locate your pond and take advantage of it, especially in summer. Spring visitors may well include spawning frogs, toads and newts. As with other habitats, a good mixture of the right kinds of vegetation is really important, both for keeping the water clean and for providing pond creatures with hiding or breeding places (*see* pages 36–9 and 76–7).

Grassland

You may not think of your lawn as much of a wildlife habitat, but if you let a small patch of it grow long you may be surprised at what you find. Long grass is very attractive to numerous insects, from certain kinds of bumblebee, which build their nests at the base of grass clumps, to meadow brown butterflies, whose caterpillars feed on grass. Some kinds of grassland in the wild also contain an amazing number of

Wildflowers growing in long grass look beautiful in early summer and will attract a whole host of insects.

different plant species. Sadly, much of this flower-rich grassland – hay meadows and chalk downland, for example – has now been lost to arable farming, like the North American prairie, but the fragments that remain show what a rich habitat the best grasslands can be. An unmown lawn may produce a far greater variety of different plants than you might expect – provided you haven't been too zealous with the weedkiller.

Starve your soil

The best flower-rich grasslands rely on poor soil, which prevents the grasses from growing strongly

A small pond near the house will draw wildlife in close, and is fascinating to watch, whether outdoors in summer, or from the window on a winter's day.

enough to overwhelm the flowers. This is one reason why meadows can be difficult to make in gardens: gardeners past and present may have spent much effort on creating lovely rich garden soil. A meadow needs the very opposite conditions. The more vigorous grasses are also unwanted in a meadow, and they, too, are common in most gardens, arriving in grass-seed mixtures for hard-wearing lawns. Serious meadow-making often involves removing tons of rich topsoil and introducing plants into the less fertile layer beneath, but unless you're really keen it should be possible to create something resembling a mini-meadow in your garden without going to such lengths (*see* pages 40–1).

Scrub

A rather unlovely name for what can in fact be a very rich wildlife habitat, scrub is, nevertheless, a useful word to describe areas of shrub-based vegetation. You don't need to turn your garden into something resembling a piece of wasteland, though. Think more in terms of a Mediterranean hillside. A garden with a variety of shrubby cover, even if trees are in short supply, can meet the needs of a range of creatures, providing undisturbed cover for nesting birds and winter quarters for ladybirds and spiders, as well as places for small mammals and amphibians to hide from predators.

Think what each plant will offer to birds and insects at each season before making your final selection.

Thorny shrubs make nests and roosting sites safer from cats and other predators. Wild roses have thorns and also flowers and hips; blackthorn and wild plums offer abundant spring nectar and winter fruits, while buckthorn will feed brimstone butterfly caterpillars. Include a few evergreens, such as holly, for shelter in winter, and ivy, for autumn nectar and winter fruits. Spindle (*Euonymus europaeus*), wayfaring tree (*Viburnum lantana*), guelder rose (*Viburnum opulus*) and elder (*Sambucus nigra*) all have blossom followed by berries that not only feed birds in winter but also give a lift to the autumn garden. If there isn't room to grow them all as freestanding shrubs, you can include them in a mixed hedge.

Go with the flow

If you're making a new garden and wondering how to plan it and what to plant, it's worth considering the wider habitat that your wildlife garden could become part of. For example, if you are close to a piece of woodland, or even some mature parkland trees, woodland birds and insects won't have far to travel and may be ready and waiting to colonize your patch if you can furnish them with what they need. Providing a log pile for insects, and peanut feeders for birds such as woodpeckers and tits, will be a good start while you wait for tree cover to develop. Likewise if there is a river, or marshland, or even several garden ponds nearby, it will be worth making a pond or bog garden to see what turns up of its own accord: this may range from frogs and newts in search of new spawning grounds, to the seeds of some attractive wetland plants.

Late-season colour, scrubby cover for wildlife and plenty to interest birds, bees and butterflies will help this border to earn its keep all year.

Choosing and buying plants

Most wildlife gardeners settle for a mixture of garden plants and native wildflowers in their plot. Buying garden plants is second nature to most keen gardeners but tracking down wildflower plants and seeds has always been a bit more of a challenge. Fortunately these are becoming more widely available at garden centres, but you may still need to go to a specialist nursery for anything out of the ordinary, and at the same time you can get expert advice on how to grow it.

Plug plants are a neat compromise: less costly than mature plants, but faster and more reliable than seed.

Where to buy

Until quite recently, gardeners wanting wildflowers had no option but to grow them from seed that had to be ordered from a specialist supplier. This could be a slow process: not all wildflowers are quick or even easy to grow from seed. Now, many garden centres are responding to rising consumer demand by stocking wild plants, and some of the big seed companies are also offering a range of wildflowers. An increasing number of specialists are also marketing native plants and seed mixes to suit farmers, landscapers and gardeners. Search online, and you'll soon see that growing wildflowers seems to be catching on in a big way!

It's a long step from a parcel of plants to an established perennial meadow, but once you get it right, it should go from strength to strength.

Wildflower plugs

Many plants that are easy to grow once established can be tricky in the early stages, and that includes certain wildflowers. Their seed may have a short shelf life; it may need pre-chilling or be otherwise hard to germinate; or the seedlings may be quick to make a tap root that won't tolerate transplanting. Buying plants as plugs avoids some of these problems, and can be a very good way of establishing wildflowers, especially in areas of grass where germinating seedlings can soon be overwhelmed. With plugs, the infant plants are already rooted into a small amount of compost. They can be sent, carefully packed, by post, and suffer less stress when transplanted. They are also cheaper to produce and transport than pot-grown plants, so if you need a lot of plants for quick impact in a meadow area, for example, they need not be prohibitively costly. Look online for companies that specialize in wildflower plugs. Before ordering, check that the plants have been responsibly sourced and grown from native seed.

Trial run

An economical approach, especially if you aren't in a hurry, is to buy just a few plugs each of several wildflower species. Let them flower

Natives or aliens?

There has been much debate recently as to the respective roles, in wildlife gardening, of native plants and garden plants that originated in other parts of the world. Undoubtedly, a varied mixture of more or less any garden plants will have considerable benefits to wildlife: providing nectar and pollen, for example, and attracting small insects such as aphids and flies, which in turn provide food for larger creatures.

Conservationists tend to favour native plants, especially in the case of trees: native species of oak, birch and willow seem to attract more different kinds of insects than their foreign relatives. The case against certain invasive alien plants is very strong: they have escaped by various means from gardens into the wider environment, where they cause not only structural damage but also displace native species by overwhelming them or interbreeding with them. Japanese knotweed (*Fallopia japonica*) and the purple-flowered *Rhododendron ponticum* are among the most notorious examples, but others, such as Himalayan balsam (*Impatiens glandulifera*) and even certain cotoneasters and the Spanish bluebell (*Hyacinthoides hispanica*), are causing concern in some places. The websites of conservation bodies such as Plantlife (www.plantlife.org.uk) are a good source of up-to-date information if you want to find out more.

For wildlife gardeners there is no simple answer, and most of us settle for some kind of compromise. A counsel of conservationist perfection might be to use only native plants that have been responsibly sourced from your own locality, but this is very restrictive, and availability is a problem. However, you should certainly avoid growing invasive pond plants (*see* page 77) and other known 'thugs'.

Spanish bluebells

English bluebells

and self-seed, and by the following year you'll be able to tell which ones suit your conditions best. You can then buy more of the most suitable ones, confident that they will succeed. Alternatively, continue to let them spread in your garden by self-seeding or by collecting and scattering the fresh seed yourself. You can even sow the seed in modules to make your own plugs for stress-free transplanting when the young plants are big enough.

Trees and shrubs

It can still be hard to obtain native shrubs and trees in garden centres. Bare-root hedging and other plants are widely available by mail order during the dormant season, though, and this can be a very inexpensive way to grow native shrubs and even trees. A year in a large pot or in the ground will see them double in size, and before you know it they will be just as tall as more mature (and costlier) specimen plants.

Propagating plants

Once you have established some wild plants in your garden, propagating them yourself is usually very easy as well as inexpensive, and you can build up stocks of plants to give away or swap with other enthusiasts. Propagating techniques are exactly the same as for regular garden plants: some are best raised from seed, some by dividing clumps or splitting clusters of bulbs, and others by taking hardwood cuttings.

Many cottage plants (here *Lychnis coronaria*) are easy to increase from your own seed. Collect it on a dry day and store in labelled envelopes to give to friends or to sow next year.

Sowing seed

It's always satisfying to succeed with new plants grown from seed, either bought or offered to you as a swap or a gift from a fellow gardener. Some wild plants, especially fragile annuals like poppies, do not transplant well, so either grow these in plugs (*see* page 29) or sow them straight into prepared ground where you want them to flower. Try growing native trees from seed, just for fun: plant some ripe acorns or hazelnuts, or the seeds from rowan or hawthorn berries, in pots in the autumn and keep them outdoors over winter. You may be lucky enough, with patience, to produce your own bit of mixed woodland from just a handful of seeds!

Self-sowers

Of course, plants in the wild manage to reproduce themselves without your help, and it's handy if you can persuade them to do the same in the garden. All you have to do is remember not to dead-head the plants after flowering, and later thin out unwanted seedlings, perhaps moving a few to start a colony in a different place. The most successful self-seeders for your wildlife garden

Chilling seeds

Some seeds of temperate-climate plants come equipped with a secret weapon that prevents them from germinating too soon and falling victim to winter weather as tender young plants. The seeds need a period of wintry chill before they will sprout. So, some seeds that have been stored indoors over winter, including those of many trees and shrubs, but also those of some herbaceous plants like hellebores and certain primulas, may not germinate when you sow them from the packet in the spring. The easiest way round this is to sow them in the autumn in pots, then put these outdoors or in a cold frame over winter. If it's already too late to do that, then mix them with a little damp compost in a plastic bag or box and put them in the fridge for a few weeks before sowing them.

will depend on your soil and conditions. *See* the panel (below) for some to try first.

Cuttings

There are a number of wildlife-friendly shrubs that are simplicity itself to propagate from cuttings taken when they are dormant in winter. These are known as hardwood cuttings because the wood is fully ripened. Elder, dogwood and willow are the easiest plants to start with. Sometimes these will grow roots just standing in a jar of water, but the best way is to cut lengths of 15–30cm (6–12in) from a mature but vigorous stem, trim them below a leaf joint and plant them at two-thirds of their depth in a pot filled with compost or directly in the ground, in a shady spot with well-drained soil.

Some enthusiastic self-seeders

Hollyhock (*Alcea rosea*)
Cow parsley (*Anthriscus sylvestris*)
Columbine (*Aquilegia*)
Red valerian (*Centranthus ruber*)
Foxglove (*Digitalis purpurea*)
Teasel (*Dipsacus fullonum*)
Miss Willmott's ghost (*Eryngium giganteum*)
Hellebores: stinking hellebore (*Helleborus foetidus*), lenten rose (*Helleborus × hybridus*)

Ox-eye daisy (*Leucanthemum vulgare*)
Evening primrose (*Oenothera biennis*)
Poppies: field poppy (*Papaver rhoeas*), opium poppy (*Papaver somniferum*)
Cowslip (*Primula veris*)
Mullein (*Verbascum*, several species/hybrids)
Vervain (*Verbena officinalis*)
Violets: sweet violet (*Viola odorata*), dog violet (*Viola riviniana*)

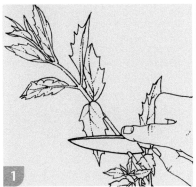

1 With a sharp knife, cut lengths of about 10cm (4in) from the ends of healthy, strong shoots. The shoots you select for propagation shouldn't be flowering.

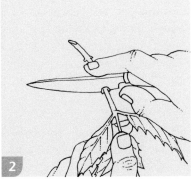

2 Trim the lower leaves from the shoot and make a cut just below a leaf joint. You should be left with an 8cm (3in) long cutting with two or three leaves.

3 Insert the cuttings around the edge of a pot of compost, using a pencil or a thin stick. Make sure the cuttings have enough space and aren't touching each other.

With many shrubs, including hebes, buddleias and caryopteris, and some perennials such as catmint and sedums, it's better to take cuttings of semi-ripe shoot-tips (*see* sequence above for guidance).

Division

Perennial wildflowers that form clumps, such as primroses and violets, may well self-sow, but a reliable way to increase your stock is to lift and divide the plants after flowering, in the same way as other herbaceous perennials. Make sure each division has some roots, replant it in improved soil, and water in well. The same techniques and timing apply to clump-forming bulbs such as snowdrops and bluebells.

Don't forget

It's illegal to dig up plants from the wild, so don't be tempted to increase your garden stocks of wildflowers that way. Why not ask friends for plants and seeds instead?

Clumps of primroses and cowslips can be split after flowering. Gently break them up into individual rosettes: each should soon make a vigorous new plant.

Hedges and boundaries

Like a hedgerow, a good mixed hedge of native species can be a fine wildlife habitat all by itself, and makes practical sense in the garden, being longer-lasting and much less expensive to install than a timber fence. Hedges provide cover for nesting and roosting birds, and winter shelter for many insects and other small creatures. They also act as 'wildlife corridors' and can provide berries for the birds, flowers for the bees, and pleasure for you as you watch their seasonal changes.

A mixed native hedge will give years of pleasure to both you and your garden wildlife. Get it off to a good start by planting in autumn, in well-prepared soil.

Establishing a hedge

Of course, hedges do take time to make a proper barrier, and that's probably why more people don't grow them. But if you prepare the ground really well with plenty of garden compost, and buy healthy, vigorous young plants, they will establish much more quickly than you may think and will soon grow away. Autumn planting is best because the plants will be well settled in by the time the growing season comes round again, whereas spring-planted hedging is much more likely to struggle in dry weather in its first summer.

Once your hedge is established, keep it within bounds by trimming once or twice a year, but don't give it a regular scalping or you will miss out on the flowers and fruits. A

Advantages of hedging

- Makes an excellent wildlife corridor (*see* page 24)
- Attractive to birds for nesting, roosting and feeding
- Winter shelter for insects and mammals
- Easier to plant in curves and irregular shapes than a wall or fence
- More attractive than most types of utility fencing
- Varied appearance through the seasons
- Wide choice of suitable plants for a variety of different situations
- Lower installation cost than fencing or walling
- No need for routine repairs or expensive replacements
- More effective at filtering wind, and more gale-resistant
- Good deterrent to burglars and vandals, especially if thorny
- Lower carbon footprint than manufactured fencing
- Filters out dust, pollution and noise
- Free from chemical preservatives

power trimmer is something you can probably manage without unless you have huge hedges. Modern shears are light and sharp, and a much greener (and quieter) option.

Fencing options

Sometimes, only a fence will do. Even a tightly clipped hedge takes up a certain amount of lateral space, so in a narrow passageway there may not be sufficient room. Elsewhere, there may not be enough soil (or any soil at all) to plant a hedge, or access for clipping may be difficult. But if it has to be fencing, don't think that your only option is the standard, brown, mass-produced panel kind. Something more rustic may suit your wildlife garden better. Look online and you may find small local companies that produce hand-crafted traditional fencing,

Dog roses capture the essence of midsummer, with colourful hips to enliven the hedge later in the year.

such as old-fashioned chestnut paling, or attractive woven fences made from willow wands, split hazel or even oak laths.

Always ask about the product's environmental credentials when buying fencing or other timber. An FSC (Forest Stewardship Council) accreditation indicates that the timber has come from sustainably managed forests.

Greening existing boundaries

Sometimes, much as you would like a hedge, you may be stuck with fencing or walling that is impossible, or impractical, or simply too wasteful to remove. There are ways and means of making your existing boundaries more appealing to wildlife (and to you too, perhaps). Climbers are an obvious solution, though they will need regular maintenance. Even a dull chain-link fence can be transformed by clipped ivy or winter jasmine, or you could grow a spring-flowering clematis through it. *Cotoneaster horizontalis* is a stalwart for growing against a wall or fence and its herringbone structure means it can be kept close to the wall without much tying-in. Birds are grateful for the berries in midwinter and bees love its little, nectar-rich flowers in late spring.

Planting to hide a fence and please birds and bees in winter: *Cotoneaster horizontalis* and *Helleborus foetidus*.

Native hedging mix

Field maple (*Acer campestre*)
Hornbeam (*Carpinus betulus*)
Dogwood (*Cornus sanguinea*)
Hawthorn (*Crataegus monogyna*)
Spindle (*Euonymus europaeus*)
Holly (*Ilex aquifolium*, evergreen)
Wild privet (*Ligustrum vulgare*)
Blackthorn (*Prunus spinosa*)
Buckthorn (*Rhamnus cathartica*)
Dog rose (*Rosa canina*)
Yew (*Taxus baccata*, evergreen)
Wayfaring tree (*Viburnum lantana*)
Guelder rose (*Viburnum opulus*)

Don't forget

Try to avoid cutting hedges in spring and early summer when birds may be nesting in them. And don't cut evergreens in winter when frost may damage them; late summer to early autumn is usually the best time.

Wildlife in small spaces

Smaller gardens are ideal for many people for all sorts of reasons, and it's perfectly possible for even the tiniest space to attract more than its fair share of wildlife. The tactics are the same as for any other garden: make your patch as inviting as possible by providing food, water and shelter. A bird table, hanging feeders, and a bird bath or small pond, all in a setting of carefully chosen, varied planting, should do the trick. None of these need take up a lot of space. Your reward will be some great close-up views of the wild visitors you attract.

Trellis with climbers is an adaptable 'quick fix' in small spaces. Use it to divide areas, to screen unsightly objects from view or to bring a wall to life with greenery and instant wildlife appeal.

Vertical space

A small garden may be short on ground space, but it has just as much vertical space as any other, and making the most of this can be key to creating a garden bursting with interest. Climbers and wall shrubs, upright evergreens such as vertical forms of yew or holly, and perhaps a tree in a container, too, will help create a permanent framework of planting to take the garden into the third dimension. Nearer to ground level, try to create layers of planting, letting tall, nectar-rich flowers such as alliums and foxgloves rise above a ground-covering blanket of perennials, including some that flower at different seasons: hardy geraniums, bugle (*Ajuga reptans*), sedums and lady's mantle (*Alchemilla mollis*) are a few to start with. Spring bulbs can be included too, providing yet another season of interest without taking up any extra space.

Versatile containers

Plants in containers are doubly useful in small spaces. You can pop them into temporary gaps in flower beds or use them to add valuable, permanent greenery to places where there's no soil, such as a balcony or roof garden, or at the base of a wall. Even in heavy shade, native evergreen ferns such as the soft shield fern (*Polystichum setiferum*) or polypody fern (*Polypodium vulgare)* will be perfectly happy, and they are no trouble to grow. Small, early bulbs such as snowdrops, crocuses and squills (*Scilla*) are good bets for small pots in sunnier spots, tempting bees and butterflies emerging from hibernation to feed on their nectar, as well as providing you with a glimpse of spring from your windows. Drought-tolerant herbs such as rosemary, lavender, sage and hyssop will provide nectar later on.

A tree undoubtedly adds something special to a garden, and there's no reason not to grow a carefully chosen

There's nothing like a well-planted balcony or roof terrace to show what can be done in next to no space.
① Densely packed planting with trees, shrubs, catmint and tulips, all flourishing in large containers, fills this decked rooftop oasis.
② In summer, osteospermums, helichrysum and a scrambling, bird-friendly *Clematis tangutica* bring colour to this city balcony.

specimen in a container, though it will demand a certain level of commitment if you are to ensure that it has everything it needs. Mainly, it mustn't dry out, particularly in spring and early summer when it is growing strongly, and it will need a yearly boost in the form of a top-dressing of compost, or being moved into a larger pot. Use a large, heavy container and a loam-based compost to help keep the whole thing stable, and choose a fairly compact variety. The snowy mespilus (*Amelanchier lamarckii*) is a good option, offering both spring blossom and autumn berries. An apple or plum is another idea; buy from a specialist and ask their advice on suitable rootstocks for growing in a pot, and also for tips

on pollination if you want your tree to fruit. If your potted tree outgrows its space, you can always give it to a friend to plant out in their garden, and start again with a different one in your own.

Add water

Water is one of the best ways of increasing your garden's attractiveness to wildlife. Even a balcony has room for a small bird bath. It should be quite shallow so that smaller birds can drink and bathe, and do remember to keep the water topped up and to clean it regularly. In a courtyard garden you might consider a wildlife pond on a tiny scale. A container such as a large, heavy ceramic or stone pot or a waterproofed wooden half-barrel (below) can work well, and is quite easy to look after. But try to fit in a decent-sized pond if you can, as larger bodies of water are less susceptible to fluctuations in temperature, and to drying out in warm weather. You don't even need a pump and filter if you introduce the right plants and other pond life such as snails (*see* page 99); they will all help keep the water clean

Size doesn't matter: there's always room for birds.
① For close encounters with feathered visitors, set up a well-stocked feeding station.
② Sparrows just love a simple, shallow bowl of water.

for you. Make sure that young froglets can climb out: carefully positioning a pile of stones or setting up a wooden ramp may be the answer.

Don't forget

It's important to include a spot where you can sit unobtrusively and enjoy your garden wildlife. A climber-clad arbour is ideal for a small garden, creating a focal point and giving height as well as a little overhead shade and a degree of camouflage. Keep still and quiet, give the birds time to get used to you being there, and you'll be surprised at just how close some of them will come.

HOW TO make a half-barrel pond

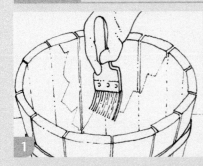

1 First clean and then scrape out any loose splinters of wood from the bottom of the barrel. Using a paintbrush and special pond paint, coat the inside of the barrel. When the first coat is dry, apply a second.

2 When the paint is completely dry, move the barrel to its final position. Either stand it on a level surface or sink it partially into the ground. Half-fill the barrel with water. Plant up the aquatic baskets (*see* page 38).

3 Different plants require different depths so arrange bricks to form 'shelves' for plant baskets. Plant stems or a projecting brick or piece of wood will help young frogs and other creatures to climb out.

Making a wildlife pond

Since many larger ponds in the town and countryside alike have disappeared, or become neglected and polluted, garden ponds have come to play an increasingly important role in the conservation of the many plant and animal species that depend on fresh water. A big pond is best if you have space, and it makes an attractive feature, but even the tiniest is better than nothing.

Dragonflies such as this broad-bodied chaser (*Libellula depressa*) are among the stars of the garden pond.

Pond practicalities

The first thing is to choose your site. It should be open and sunny, and on level ground or at the foot of a slope. Avoid overhanging trees, and leave space to walk comfortably all the way round the pond. A seat for pond watching is sure to be well used, and ideally the pond would be visible from the house, too.

For maximum wildlife appeal you'll need plenty of clean, shallow water. Make sure the edges are gently sloping for easy access and can cope with fluctuating water levels. Plan at least one area of deeper water – say 60cm (2ft) deep: ponds tend to silt up over time, and shallow ponds can soon dry up in a heatwave, or freeze solid in winter. Deeper water also gives tadpoles and other pond life a better chance of escaping from predators such as birds, which fish in the shallows.

Late winter is a good time to begin. There's no need to hurry, and everything can settle before the spring planting rush. Try to dig the hole in dry weather to avoid a sea of mud. Buy a butyl rubber liner if possible: they are expensive, but flexible and durable.

It's better not to introduce fish into a wildlife pond, especially if it is small. The tadpoles of frogs and newts, and various aquatic larvae, are all more likely to survive with no fish to gobble them up. Some fish tend to make the water muddy, too.

A sunny position, gently sloping edges and varied planting, including some native wildflowers, help make this small pond irresistible to wildlife.

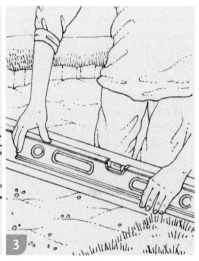

1 Once you have established the shape of your pond using a hosepipe or a length of rope, mark the perimeter by pouring dry sand from a plastic bottle. Decide where you want deeper areas, and keep edges shallow for easy access. Avoid steep gradients above and below the water.

2 If you're fairly fit, dig the area by hand. It's cheaper and less disruptive than a mini-digger and can be done a bit at a time. Remove and stack any turf that you want to keep for edging the pond. Dump the spoil on a large tarpaulin or in a nearby wheelbarrow to cart away.

3 Take time to make sure that the rim of the pond is level all the way round. Move soil by building the edges up or bringing the level down until the edge looks level, then check that it is by placing a spirit level on a long plank across the top of the hole. Repeat in other places around the edge.

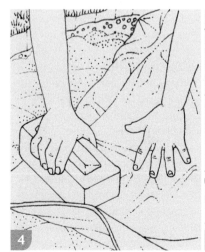

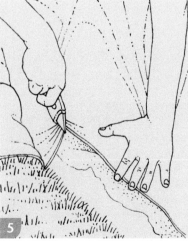

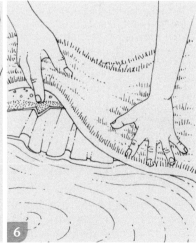

4 Remove stones from the surface of the hole and spread an even layer of soft sand 25mm (1in) thick over it. Cover the sand with pond underlay and peg the edges in place. Then centre the pond liner over the hole, unfold it and ease it into place. Anchor the edges temporarily with bricks.

5 Fill the pond with a hose or, better still, with rainwater. As it fills, adjust the liner to hug the shape of the hole, forming small, neat folds. Leave the whole thing to settle overnight, then trim the edges of the liner, leaving an excess of 30cm (12in) beyond the edge of the water.

6 Cover the exposed edges of the liner so it won't perish in the sun. Turf, plants or a 'beach' of pebbles or slate chippings are natural-looking options for a wildlife pond, allowing birds and other creatures to reach the water easily. Begin to introduce plants when the water has had time to settle.

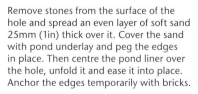

Planting in and around a wildlife pond

Planting is critical to the success of a wildlife pond, so be generous. The right plants will help keep the water clean and fulfil one of the chief requirements of visiting creatures: a place to hide from predators, both in the water and on their way to and from it. It's a harsh world out there.

Plants of different types fulfil different roles in the life of a pond and its visitors. Choose as many native plants as possible (*see* pages 76–7), with a wide range, from floating plants to wildflowers that thrive in the grass around a pond.

Many submerged plants, such as curled pondweed (*Potamogeton crispus*), contribute vital oxygen to

In a new pond, purpose-made planting baskets can help plants to establish. Anchor the plants firmly into the planting medium and top-dress with grit or gravel.

Tips for planting success

■ Make sure the pond has a good mixture of submerged and marginal plants, with plenty of cover around its edges (*see* pages 76–7).

■ To make a shallow area in a deep pond, section off an area with loose stones or bricks. Add some washed shingle or silver sand behind the barrier and anchor marginal plants into that. They will soon grow new roots into it.

■ Put in pond plants in late spring, when water temperatures are high enough for them to grow away and establish fast.

help keep the pond fresh. Then there are deep-water plants, for example the native white water lily *Nymphaea alba*, and marginal plants such as water mint, bog bean and brooklime for the shallows. These all like to have their roots submerged but their leaves above the surface. There's an even greater choice of wildflowers for the surrounds of the pond, and they will look much more natural if you choose plants that grow close to water in the wild.

Water quality

Whatever the size of your pond, the most important thing is to make sure the water is kept clean. In a wildlife pond, no pump or filter should be necessary. Once you have the right balance of plants and other pond life working well, nature can be left largely to its own devices – though you should be on the alert for any warning signs that all is not well, especially in warm weather,

Keeping your pond sweet

■ Try to prevent runoff into the pond from neighbouring bare soil. Keeping adjacent areas covered with planting or grass will help.

■ Never use fertilizers (including lawn fertilizer) near a garden pond.

■ When adding pond plants, use a heavy, nutrient-poor planting medium such as sandy loam rather than fertilizer-rich potting compost.

■ Remove blanket weed and duckweed as and when you see them.

■ Set up a water butt to take runoff from a roof, and use this rather than tap water to top up your pond when necessary.

A 'beach' of pebbles is an ideal pond edging, giving wild creatures easy access to the water and shielding the pond liner from the sun.

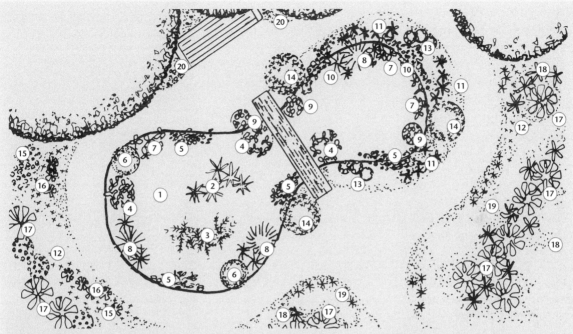

Deeper water

1 Curled pondweed (*Potamogeton crispus*) (x 5)
2 Water soldier (*Stratiotes aloides*) (x 1)
3 Water violet (*Hottonia palustris*) (x 1)

Shallow water

4 Blue flag (*Iris versicolor*) (x 3)
5 Water mint (*Mentha aquatica*) (x 3)
6 Water forget-me-not (*Myosotis scorpioides*) (x 2)

7 Bog bean (*Menyanthes trifoliata*) (x 3)
8 Flowering rush (*Butomus umbellatus*) (x 3)
9 Kingcup (*Caltha palustris*) (x 3)
10 Brooklime (*Veronica beccabunga*) (x 2)

Pond edges

11 Ragged robin (*Lychnis flos-cuculi*) (x 15)
12 Snakeshead fritillary (*Fritillaria meleagris*) (x 50)
13 Water avens (*Geum rivale*) (x 6)
14 Meadowsweet (*Filipendula ulmaria*) (x 3)

Naturalized in grass

15 Meadow buttercup (*Ranunculus acris*) (x 5)
16 Cuckoo flower (*Cardamine pratensis*) (x 10)
17 Ox-eye daisy (*Leucanthemum vulgare*) (x 12)
18 Cowslip (*Primula veris*) (x 20)
19 Yellow rattle (*Rhinanthus minor*) (x 20)
20 Wood anemone (*Anemone blanda*) (x 50)

Looking after your pond

Once your garden pond is established, with a good balance of plants and other pond life, it shouldn't need frequent maintenance. Keep an eye on the water level, though. It's fine if it fluctuates to some extent, but if it drops too low in dry weather, top the pond up. If some plants are really threatening to take over, thin them out at the end of summer and remove seedheads. After a few years, you may need to clean out some of the accumulated debris from the bottom of the pond. Do this during a mild spell in winter, well before breeding frogs are likely to arrive. Pile up any plants or other material that you have removed by the side of the pond and leave them there overnight to allow captured creatures to make their way back to the water.

A WILDLIFE POND AND SURROUNDS
AREA 7.5 x 5M (25 x 16FT); POND LENGTH 4.5M (15FT)

The 'waisted' shape of this pond allows for separate deep and shallow areas, each with appropriate plants. The water is spanned at its narrowest point by a simple bridge made of stout oak planks, to add structure and interest. A grassy path runs all the way round the pond's edge, and there is a sunny seat for pond watching.

and be ready to remedy the situation as quickly as you can.

Fertile soil may be just the thing for your cabbages, but nutrients are the last thing you want in a pond. They promote the growth of algae and blanket weed, which can adversely affect oxygen levels in the water and make it unpleasantly murky. It's true that some freshwater creatures can tolerate a certain amount of pollution (otherwise the poor state of many ponds might have wiped out far more of them), but you will have a wider range of pond life in clean water, and it looks much nicer too. *See* Keeping your pond sweet (opposite) for some tips.

Grass, lawns and meadows

Well-kept turf can look great, and blackbirds, thrushes and starlings like to search for earthworms, beetle larvae and moth chrysalises just below the surface of short grass and also catch ants above it. Birds will even help you with lawn maintenance by eating turf pests such as leatherjackets. An immaculate lawn, however, isn't the best wildlife habitat, and there are ways to use grass more imaginatively. But relax … you certainly don't need to turn your lawn into a full-scale hay meadow.

Grass for wildlife

There are two main ways of making grass more attractive to wildlife. One is to mix grasses with other plants to create a wildflower lawn. Allowing a few low-growing, flowering 'weeds', such as clover, bird's-foot trefoil, daisies and self-heal, to remain in a sunny area of lawn can look pretty, once you get used to the idea, and it will soon begin to attract insects and

perhaps also seed-eating birds. Planting small, early-flowering bulbs (*see* right) that will attract bees to their nectar on sunny days is another option. A flowering lawn doesn't demand dramatic changes to your mowing habits: simply start cutting the grass a little later in the season, cut it less frequently, and raise the mower blades to leave it slightly longer, say 5cm (2in).

Low perennials for a wildflower lawn

Daisy (*Bellis perennis*)

Bird's-foot trefoil (*Lotus corniculatus*)

Self-heal (*Prunella vulgaris*)

Red clover (*Trifolium pratense*)

Germander speedwell (*Veronica chamaedrys*)

Sweet violet (*Viola odorata*)

Buying wildflowers as plugs (*see* pages 28–9) is a more reliable way to establish them in grass than sowing seed. Rooted into a small cell of soil, the plantlets are more likely to hold their own against competing grasses.

The second method is to let an area of grass grow longer, cutting it perhaps just a couple of times a year. Long grass can be a very rich wildlife habitat, providing food for the caterpillars of many butterflies and moths as well as cover for bugs, nesting bumblebees, and crickets. Allow the grasses to flower and seed, and you'll create a further food source for birds.

Flowering meadows

In large gardens, a grassy space full of flowers – cowslips and snakeshead fritillaries in spring, or ox-eye daisies later (*see* pages 72–3) – brings joy to people and insects alike. When making a meadow like this, the main challenge is preventing the grass from overwhelming the flowers. If you are creating a meadow from scratch, it's far more likely to succeed on poor soil, where the lack of nutrients will limit the spread of the grasses. You can also select finer grasses, avoiding the tough and vigorous species that are included in lawn mixes. And you can plant yellow rattle (*Rhinanthus minor, see* page 73), which is semi-parasitic so keeps some thuggish grasses in check. Depending on what kind of soil you have to begin with, these measures may reduce the soil fertility sufficiently for a meadow to work. If not, you might have to move the rich topsoil elsewhere and start again.

When and how to mow

Cut your meadow grass as soon as the latest-blooming flowers have finished and set seed. If these are cowslips, you'll be able to cut soon after midsummer; if they are

A mown, curving path and a planned focal point (here, a small wooden gate framed by trees) help give a flowering meadow essential structure all year.

later-flowering knapweeds, wild carrot and scabious, leave the grass until early autumn. Your meadow may not look its best at this stage in the season, especially if the plants are battered by rain and wind, but your patience will be rewarded the following year.

Most ordinary mowers aren't suited to cutting really long grass. A small mini-meadow can be given its first cut with shears: these are better than a strimmer, as there's less risk of harming creatures like frogs or slow-worms. For a large-scale meadow, it may be a good idea to

hire a power scythe. Whichever cutting method you use, remember to rake up all the grass so that it doesn't decompose and add unwanted nutrients to the soil. The grass will look dead to begin with, but it will usually begin to green up within a couple of weeks of cutting.

Don't forget

Longer grass in the garden can easily give the impression that you've simply neglected to mow. Avoid this by keeping some closely mown paths through the longer grass. It will give shape and purpose to the whole area – and you won't get wet feet.

Maintaining a wildlife-friendly garden

When it comes to maintenance, wildlife gardening certainly allows a relaxed approach, but don't for a moment imagine you can hang up your tools and put your feet up for good. Keeping a balanced mix of flora and fauna means not letting the thugs take over, so you'll sometimes have to intervene to make sure not only that plants and animals have enough light and air, but also that your garden continues to look attractive.

Weeding

It's worth almost any amount of trouble to eradicate troublesome perennial weeds such as ground elder and bindweed from your planned wildlife garden before you plant anything. Don't be tempted to leave them as part of nature's rich tapestry, because they make it very difficult to grow other plants nearby with their invasive ways and greedy habits, and they can be incredibly difficult to dig out from among other plants later.

You can be a bit more relaxed about less tyrannical weeds, and you may even come to love some of them: many are very pretty, after all. But be ready to deal with anything that tries to swamp its neighbours as soon as your back is turned. Even in a wild garden you must sometimes be ruthless in order to keep the planting varied. And remember that self-sown seedlings will make better plants if they aren't overcrowded.

Mulching with leaf mould or home-made compost (*see* pages 54–5) helps to keep annual weeds to a manageable level. It also feeds the plants and helps them retain moisture – not to mention keeping soil organisms busy and therefore promoting healthy soil.

Beds and borders

Some would-be wildlife gardeners may be disappointed to learn that very tidy gardens aren't good for wildlife, but a few simple changes are often all it takes to make a

Don't be in a hurry to cut down perennials that have flowered. Some seedheads, like these sedums, can be left standing until early spring.

garden wildlife-friendly. Tidying flower borders in spring rather than autumn is one way of adapting your gardening habits to suit wildlife. A bed that is groomed to a squeaky-clean state by October won't offer much winter shelter or food, but if you must have tidy borders for the winter, include a few compact evergreen shrubs to act as wildlife shelters. Also plant some strong, weather-resistant perennials, such as *Sedum* 'Herbstfreude' or *Phlomis russeliana*, to leave standing when you cut the rest down. Their seedheads will make structural features and provide many birds and insects with winter accommodation and food. A winter blanket of lovely dark mulch will help protect plants and make a wonderful setting for the emerging flowers of snowdrops and hellebores in the new year.

Use wire netting and posts to make a simple container for dead leaves, which will rot down to produce a valuable soil conditioner.

Winter quarters

Before disposing of the plants you have chopped down, consider cutting some of the hollow stems into shorter lengths and tying them in bundles to tuck into a hedge or some other out-of-the-way spot. They will make an unobtrusive winter hotel for ladybirds, spiders and other invertebrates.

Pruning and trimming

Most work on deciduous trees and shrubs, such as pruning, trimming and coppicing, is best done when they're dormant in winter. It's better for the plant, and you needn't worry about disturbing nesting birds. But problems caused by a shrub that has outgrown its space don't seem half as pressing when its branches are bare, so plan any pruning the previous summer – only when a shrub or climber is in full leaf do you appreciate how much light it is

If you have more than one buddleia, stagger the pruning over several weeks so that some will flower later. This will provide nectar for butterflies and bees over a longer season.

taking from a neighbour. Exceptions to winter pruning include plums and cherries (*Prunus*), which should be pruned when the sap is flowing and they are less likely to pick up disease through the cuts. With shrubs that flower early in the season, including forsythia, lilac, philadelphus and weigela, it's best if you remove some old branches after flowering, but check carefully for nests first.

Birds will normally have finished nesting by late summer, and that's the best time to do most of your hedge cutting, particularly with evergreens such as yew and box. You'll catch most of the current year's growth, and any further new shoots will have time to harden off before frosts return.

Feeding the birds

A good wildlife garden will be rich in 'natural' food to suit a whole range of visiting birds: a healthy population of aphids, caterpillars and other insects; other invertebrates such as worms and woodlice; and a variety of seeds and berries. But supplies of these food sources will fluctuate during the course of the year, and most people with an interest in garden birds like to provide supplementary food, too.

Shopping for birds

A whole industry has now grown up to supply a huge range of special foods that are adapted to the needs of different birds, together with all sorts of contraptions to dispense it (some more practical than others). You can buy these in pet shops, DIY stores, garden centres and online. But you don't need to spend a fortune or buy elaborate ornamental feeders to do the best for your birds. Just remember to keep them regularly supplied with a variety of nutritious foods – and don't forget they need water too.

Safe feeding

Any place where small birds gather in large numbers is likely to become a target for predators such as cats and sparrowhawks, and you should be prepared for attacks because it's often difficult to keep either of these out of your garden. Siting feeders or nest boxes at a high level makes them less accessible to cats. A thorny shrub or hedge beneath can help, but remember that you'll need access to refill feeders without getting scratched. Where birds feed on the ground or at a bird table, dense, low vegetation near by can too easily provide a hiding place for a cat on the prowl. Trees offer small birds the safest cover.

Don't forget

Once you begin providing for your garden birds, they will come to rely on you. Try not to let them down by forgetting to fill feeders or allowing food and water to run out when you're away. This applies throughout the year, but it's especially important in winter: birds can use a lot of energy travelling to sources of food and water, so make sure they don't have a wasted journey to your feeding station.

Uncomplicated seed feeders tend to be the best. Clean them out thoroughly every couple of weeks.

Peanuts

Hanging up a peanut feeder is an easy and rewarding way to access the world of garden wildlife. You'll seldom have to wait long for the first blue tits to turn up, and they're likely to be followed by great tits, greenfinches, chaffinches, house sparrows, perhaps a great spotted woodpecker or even a nuthatch. A gang of ground-feeding opportunists including dunnocks and collared doves will soon arrive to clear up the bits the others drop. Start with a basic feeder, but be prepared to upgrade it to a sturdier model if it attracts unwelcome attention from squirrels or sparrowhawks. Nut feeders should have mesh small enough to prevent birds taking away whole nuts, which could choke their young. Stored peanuts can become contaminated with a mould that is poisonous to birds, so always buy from a reputable source and keep them somewhere dry and cool.

Seeds

A varied seed mixture will suit many different bird species, but be selective because some seed mixtures are much better than others. Avoid mixes that contain a lot of wheat: they may be cheap, but they appeal chiefly to pigeons and collared doves. Sunflower seeds, either on their own or as part of a mixture, will be popular with finches and tits. You can buy them either whole, as black sunflower seeds, or with their husks removed, as sunflower hearts – more expensive, but easier for the birds to eat, and less messy. Seeds are best dispensed in a special seed feeder, hung where you can easily clear up underneath to prevent dropped food turning mouldy and attracting bacteria.

Fruit

Blackbirds and thrushes love fruit and will be attracted to fallen apples, especially when the weather turns cold, and to all sorts of garden berries including those of yew, pyracanthas and cotoneasters. If you're lucky, the fruit will also attract winter-visiting fieldfares and redwings. And a great year-round treat for your blackbirds, if you really want to make friends with them, is a handful of dried fruit, such as sultanas. They like them so much that in time they may come to the window and 'ask' for them. Keep a jar handy by the door!

Kitchen scraps

Commercial bird food may be more nutritious, but small amounts of kitchen scraps on the bird table will do no harm, and birds seem to enjoy the variety. Grated cheese, suet and other fats, oats, bread and cake crumbs, and cooked rice will all be

Adult birds, such as this great tit, can tackle whole peanuts in the shell, but a wire-mesh nut holder is better in spring, when they are feeding young.

appreciated. Avoid any food that is going off and anything salty, and don't put out too much starchy food. Enthusiasts can make their own 'bird cake' by mixing seeds, nuts and crumbs with melted fat and pouring it into a container such as an empty half-coconut or special 'tit bell'. Hang it up and watch them tuck in.

Blackbirds enjoy many kinds of fruit such as apples and berries, but raisins and sultanas are particular favourites.

Don't forget

Where large numbers of birds congregate, diseases and bacteria can build up all too readily. Scrub bird tables, bird baths and feeders regularly, using hot soapy water, and rinse well. (Wear rubber gloves, and take care not to let the water splash into your eyes.) Move feeders to a fresh site from time to time, too, to prevent droppings accumulating.

Housing your visitors

Once your garden is on the local wildlife radar and attracting regular visitors to feed, longer-term residents may well be only a short step away. It's always a great thrill when a bird decides to raise a family in your garden, and you can help things along by providing suitable places – both natural and man-made – where they can build their nests. The same applies to many other wild creatures you may want to attract into your garden.

You're more likely to hear tawny owls in your garden than to see one, but they just may be tempted by a good roosting site or a suitable nest box.

Natural havens

Good, safe cover is essential for many birds to feel secure enough to use your garden for breeding. Dense hedges and shrubs are popular with blackbirds, chaffinches and robins. Goldfinches, greenfinches and mistle thrushes are among the birds that prefer trees. Blue tits, great tits and coal tits like holes in old trees.

Remember that all the birds that visit your garden by day must find places to shelter and keep warm at night. Starlings are well known for their noisy communal roosts, and larger birds like pigeons and rooks perch in trees. In cold weather, smaller species such as wrens and tits will huddle together for warmth, choosing a well-protected place such as a hedge or climber-clad wall.

A climber planted against a house or garage wall will also provide a wonderful shelter for overwintering ladybirds and spiders, and perhaps for small birds to nest in, too. Before attaching trellis panels, fix wooden battens to the wall. The extra space that is created allows more depth of planting, which will, in turn, protect sheltering insects as well as roosting and nesting birds. Choose climbers with birds and insects in mind: honeysuckle has both nectar and berries, and some kinds of clematis, for instance *Clematis alpina* or *Clematis tangutica* (*see* left), have fluffy seedheads that birds can use as nesting material.

Plants growing against warm, south-facing walls bring spring forward because they flower earlier. Fragrant, blossoming shrubs please bees, and fill the air with sweet scent on sunny days: try *Daphne bholua*,

white forsythia (*Abeliophyllum distichum*) or flowering quince (*Chaenomeles speciosa*). Even a north-facing wall can support a berrying shrub. *Cotoneaster horizontalis* is an easy one for sun or shade, reliably producing nectar-rich flowers and a midwinter berry feast. Pyracanthas are more vigorous, but look wonderful when laden with yellow, orange or red berries.

In and around buildings

Don't underestimate the wildlife potential of your house. Not everyone wants to share their living accommodation – especially with the creatures that seem keenest to move in, such as mice and house spiders. But with a little help, the outside of your buildings can become a valuable habitat.

Clematis tangutica is a vigorous, sun-loving scrambler. The fluffy seedheads provide winter interest as well as sought-after nesting material.

Don't forget

If you sometimes find dead or injured birds that have flown into your window panes, fix some purpose-made bird silhouette stickers on the glass, to help prevent future casualties.

Sometimes, birds nest in and around buildings. Robins and wrens may make theirs in sheds and garages, perhaps in an old hat or kettle; house sparrows and starlings often seek out cavities in roofs and walls. Nests of swallows and house martins are often found under eaves. These birds are now in decline all over Europe owing to reduced numbers of farmyards, which once supplied the barns, the mud and the insects that these graceful birds need for nesting and feeding. You can help them by erecting special cup-shaped nest boxes or shelves beneath the eaves of your house or garage. Provide a muddy place for building material, too: each pair of birds needs hundreds of pellets of soft mud to make a whole nest. If successful, they may produce two broods in a good season.

House martins' nests are a marvel of engineering. Built up gradually, using many beakfuls of mud, they stay put all summer – and sometimes longer.

Bats also roost and breed in buildings, especially if cracks and crevices give them access to lofts and other undisturbed spaces. If you see bats around, have a look for signs of them in your roof space, although you're more likely to see their droppings than the bats themselves. It's illegal to disturb bat roosts, and why would you want to anyway? They are completely harmless, and they devour some of the flies, gnats and mosquitoes that might otherwise bother you on summer evenings.

Purpose-built homes

Loss of habitat, particularly the trend towards smaller, tidier gardens featuring hard landscaping, is thought to be a factor in the decline of several once-common garden animals. You can improve the situation by making or buying suitable homes for them to roost, hibernate or breed in.

Smaller creatures, such as solitary bees, ladybirds and lacewings, like to hide away in dark, dry nooks and crannies. You can buy special shelters for these creatures, but many are easy to make yourself, from a simple bundle of bamboo canes to a full-scale 'insect hotel' made from wood, bricks, tiles, moss, straw and leaf litter (see page 103).

Hedgehogs may also be encouraged to move into your garden. They like dense vegetation, a dark shelter, and plenty of dry material for bedding. More sophisticated hedgehog fans may like to buy or make a special wooden box for them to hibernate or breed in. The best ones are rather like a small dog kennel but darker and more snug, preferably with a tunnel for an entrance. If you want to make your own hedgehog box you'll find detailed guidance online.

Nesting materials

Birds, hedgehogs and other creatures that may be tempted to build their nests in your garden will be more enthusiastic if they regard you as a handy builders' merchant. Twigs, grass, moss and lichen, cobwebs, leaves and mud are among the most commonly used nesting materials, and all these are likely to be found in your garden if you aren't obsessive about tidiness. Some plants provide perfect bedding material, particularly those with fluffy seedheads that overwinter (see opposite). You may even like to provide your birds with tailor-made bundles of nesting material, such as small bits of wool, paper and hair. Hang these up in a loose-meshed string bag to allow the birds to pull out whatever they fancy.

Don't forget

Jackdaws sometimes nest in chimneys, which can have dangerous consequences. If you have an open-topped chimney and there are jackdaws in your area, before you light a fire check the chimney – twigs may have been dropped down it by hopeful birds.

Make a hedgehog den by covering a weatherproof box with twigs or dead leaves.

Putting up a well-insulated, wedge-shaped bat box may encourage bats to set up home in your garden.

Bat boxes

Since bat populations are on the decline, it is helpful to encourage bats to roost and breed in your garden by providing a bat box. Bats like roosting sites that are well-insulated and draughtproof, so bat boxes need to be well made if they are to succeed. It isn't difficult to make one, but it's important to get the dimensions right and to position it properly. There is a lot of detailed information about how to do this on the internet.

Wedge-shaped boxes seem to be the most successful, with a fixed roof, weatherproof joints, a landing area and an opening at the bottom that is big enough to admit the bats but not predators. Rough-sawn timber will help the bats to grip the inside of the box with their amazing toes, and it's important that the timber is untreated.

Whether you make or buy a bat box, site it high in a tree or on a building, in a position where it will get the sun for at least part of the day, but not facing into prevailing winds. The bats need a clear approach to the box.

Nest boxes for birds

Blue tits and great tits are among the likeliest occupants of nest boxes, but several other species may also use them. Basic boxes with a removable front can be adapted to suit particular species. In fact, some nest boxes are sold with different front panels so you can choose between a completely enclosed box with a round access hole, and an open-fronted box with a half-panel for the front. If you make your own boxes, a range of refinements to suit different species is possible (see panel, below).

Give careful thought to the positioning of nest boxes. They should not be in full sun, nor facing into strong, wet westerly winds. East and north are the best aspects. They should be at least 2m (6ft) from the ground. Set the boxes up well before the breeding season begins in spring, to allow birds the chance to explore and get used to them. And remember to clean out previously used nest boxes in winter, removing old nesting material and debris in good time for the new season.

Birds and boxes	
BIRD	BOX REQUIREMENTS
Robin	Open-fronted box
Wren	Open-fronted box
Blue tit, coal tit	Box with hole 25mm (1in) in diameter
Great tit	Box with hole 28mm (1⅛in)
House sparrow, nuthatch	Box with hole 32mm (1¼in)
Starling	Box with hole 45mm (1¾in)

Different shapes and sizes of nest box are likely to attract blue tits, great tits and other species, too. If you have space, try several in different places.

Green or 'living' roofs covered with specially adapted planting are most often seen on big new buildings, but they can work well on a garden shed or the flat top of an extension or a garage. A living roof is a good way to increase the green area of a small garden, and the planting can be chosen for wildlife appeal: some tough native flowers, particularly those that thrive in poor soils, are well suited to the harsh conditions of rooftop life.

Greening a roof

Building a green roof needs thought. Most importantly, it will be heavy, so the building must be sturdy enough to support the weight. Get professional advice if in doubt, and install additional timber supports and bracing if necessary. The roof should be flat or gently sloping, and must also be properly watertight. Excess water must be able to drain away, too.

If this all sounds daunting, just think of a green roof as a shallow container filled with tough, easy plants. If you're hesitant about committing yourself to a

Planting a green roof

You can sow seed, insert plug plants, or buy ready-planted matting that you roll out like turf, which is the easiest but most expensive option. Suitable plants will depend on the depth of the growing medium, but just 5–10cm (2–4in) will support a colourful native wildflower mixture that might include biting stonecrop (*Sedum acre*), bird's-foot trefoil (*Lotus corniculatus*), cowslip (*Primula veris*), rock rose (*Helianthemum*), wild thyme (*Thymus polytrichus*) and various hawkweeds (*Pilosella*) and vetches (*Vicia*). Other low-growing possibilities include dwarf sedums and pinks (*Dianthus*), houseleeks (*Sempervivum*), *Acaena* and some kinds of saxifrage.

A green roof can utilize 'dead space' to boost your garden's wildlife potential. If possible, create one where you can see it from your upstairs windows.

full-scale green roof, experiment on a small structure, for example a pet hutch or even a bird-table roof, to give you confidence. Start with a shallow depth of planting medium, up to 5cm (2in), and use indestructible plants like sedums and houseleeks. Materials such as man-made landscape fabric, and light, expanded-clay granules for planting, will help minimize weight.

Green roofs: what lies beneath

A living roof is built in layers. Systems vary, but these may include:

1 A waterproof base layer, like a pond liner, essential to prevent plants damaging the roof of the building.

2 A drainage layer of gravel or other coarse granular material, with plenty of air spaces.

3 A filter layer of semi-permeable landscape fabric to prevent soil particles being washed away.

4 A top layer of low-fertility growing medium: a small proportion of soil or compost mixed with aggregate such as limestone chippings or crushed waste brick or concrete.

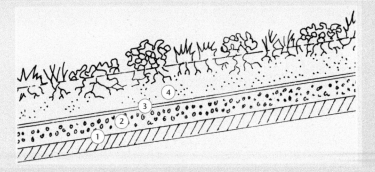

Unwelcome visitors

Not every visitor that chooses to move into your garden will receive an equally warm welcome. Some of them may cause unacceptable levels of damage, while others may kill or injure the very creatures you are proud to be sharing your garden with, such as nesting birds and their young. There are no easy solutions but there are measures you can take to discourage destructive pests without running the risk of upsetting the complex balance of the whole garden community.

Feathered nuisances

Much as we love birds in the garden, certain species can sometimes be a nuisance, especially when they damage your crops. If you don't want a full-scale fruit cage, temporary netting will keep blackbirds away from soft fruit, and pigeons off cabbages. Make sure the net is stretched taut over supports, with no trailing bits to entangle birds, and always check for holes, especially at ground level – birds may spend ages looking for a way in and then be unable to get out.

Bullfinches are exciting to see in the garden – the male, with his deep-pink breast and black head, usually accompanied by the more subtly buff-coloured female. But they may be less welcome in late winter and spring, when they snack

On the increase in many rural areas, rabbits eat a wide variety of plants. Fencing and tree guards may keep them away from your favourites.

on the fattening buds of your fruit trees. Pigeons, too, may eat the buds, blossom and young leaves of cherry trees. Netting whole trees is usually impractical: discourage the birds by hanging moving, shiny objects such as unwanted CDs in the trees for a week or two.

Ripening tree-fruit such as cherries and plums can be protected from blackbirds by slipping tubes of a light, porous fabric such as old net curtains or horticultural fleece loosely over the branches that have the best crops of berries.

A bold, visiting fox is charm itself to watch, and may cause no real problems in large, rural gardens. However, owners of city gardens where foxes have taken up residence may feel less well disposed towards these beguiling but sometimes messy and destructive animals.

Deterrents to try

Cats, rabbits, mice and other animals can sometimes be persuaded to go elsewhere. Try the following simple and harmless temporary deterrents:

■ Prickly prunings such as holly or hawthorn laid around vulnerable plants.

■ A well-aimed water pistol or squeezy plastic bottle filled with water.

■ Shiny foil or CDs, hung up on string so they can move easily in the wind and reflect light. Or stick children's windmills (the sort you buy at the seaside) in the soil. Move both types around regularly: most animals tend to dislike change and are suspicious of anything new.

■ Purpose-made ultrasonic devices. These are quite expensive, but will be worth it if they work.

■ Small-mesh wire netting cut and bent into different shapes, making reusable protection for plants that are likely to come under attack.

■ Pepper dust, sprinkled on a dry day in areas visited by cats, rabbits and mice.

■ Lion dung pellets (yes, really – look for them online!).

Netting is a simple way to keep pigeons off your cabbages. Secure it tightly and make sure it can't accidentally entangle small birds.

Squirrels, mice and voles find some overwintering bulbs irresistible, so cover pots with wire netting to prevent disappointment in spring.

Deer and rabbits

Many rural gardeners despair at the damage caused by deer or rabbits. Purpose-built fencing is the only real solution, but it's expensive and makes your garden look forbidding unless it's well disguised. Deer fencing, in particular, isn't easy to hide as it needs to be at least 1.8m (6ft) high to stop the deer from jumping over it. The best course of action is to grow plants that deer and rabbits are unlikely to eat unless desperate (see right). And don't forget to fix guards around young trees to prevent damage to the bark.

Grey squirrels

Grey squirrels not only strip tree bark and dig up bulbs, they are also predators, taking eggs and young from birds' nests. They steal peanuts and other bird food, too, sometimes wrecking feeders in the process. Squirrels are difficult to deter but you can buy specially reinforced bird-feeding equipment that may stop them pilfering. Use tree guards to protect young saplings and bury pieces of wire netting on top of newly planted bulbs so squirrels can't dig them up.

Moles

These determined creatures can cause problems if they tunnel under a seed bed, but elsewhere they seldom cause serious damage. Fortunately moles have large territories, so after a few weeks of sweeping molehills off your lawn you may find they have moved on.

Deer- and rabbit-resistant plants

SHRUBS	Elder (Sambucus nigra)	Honesty (Lunaria annua)
Mexican orange blossom (Choisya ternata)	Christmas box (Sarcococca)	Catmint (Nepeta)
Cotoneaster	Thyme (Thymus)	Penstemon
Daphne		Mullein (Verbascum)
Bay (Laurus nobilis)	BORDER FLOWERS	
Mahonia	Monkshood (Aconitum)	BULBS
Osmanthus	Columbine (Aquilegia)	Ornamental onion (Allium)
Rosemary (Rosmarinus officinalis)	Foxglove (Digitalis)	Snowdrop (Galanthus)
Rue (Ruta graveolens)	Eryngium	Snowflake (Leucojum)
Sage (Salvia officinalis)	Eupatorium	Narcissus
	Euphorbia	Nerine
	Hellebore (Helleborus)	

Blue tits are in the vanguard of your 'garden army', gathering huge numbers of insects to feed their young. This one has a cranefly.

Traditional mole deterrents, which involve sabotaging their runs with something noisy or smelly, don't seem to work for very long. Moles are clever and rather charming creatures, and it's probably best to learn to live with them.

Cats

Cats provoke mixed feelings among gardeners – much depends on whether it's your own cat, or someone else's. They can be useful if you need to control mice and rats, but are far from welcome when they bury their waste in your seed bed, or use a newly planted tree as a scratching post. And even the most committed cat-lover can't deny the havoc that cats, generally, wreak among garden wildlife. Small mammals, slow-worms and baby birds are especially vulnerable. Cats are difficult but not impossible to deter (see page 51) and fitting a bell to your cat's collar will certainly help.

Insect pests

A busy wildlife garden is sure to contain numerous small creatures that have a taste for your plants. That's partly why they visit you, after all. Not so very long ago it was almost universally taken for granted that most of these were 'pests' to be sprayed. The beneficial insects, as often as not, died along with the miscreants. Now, attitudes are slowly changing and there's a growing reluctance among gardeners to throw out the baby with the bath water by indiscriminate use of chemicals. Legislation has removed many harmful pesticides from the shelves, and an increasing number of us would rather have a few holes in our lettuces and feel more secure about what's in the food we eat.

It's hard to be generous towards vine weevils, whose plump white larvae will soon destroy plant roots.

An established wildlife garden is unlikely to have huge pest problems because most plant-eaters have their predators, and over time a balanced community will develop. But there always seem to be troublesome creatures – often newly introduced and non-native – whose presence can make gardening particularly frustrating. At present, vine weevils and lily beetles are among the most unpopular garden pests.

Vine weevils

If a pot plant suddenly wilts inexplicably, lift it and inspect its roots for the tell-tale fat, white larvae of the vine weevil – one of the top garden pests. They are especially prevalent in damp, soilless potting compost in containers, and on primulas and heucheras in the garden, but they will attack a wide range of plants. Once a big problem in the nursery trade, they have been kept in check by specially treated compost and parasitic nematodes that work as a biological control. You can also remove the adult weevils at night, by torchlight.

Lily beetles

Another unwelcome guest is the lily beetle. The bright red adults are easy to see on the lily and fritillary plants where they feed and breed. The larvae are less obvious but distinctive, concealed under their own slimy black droppings on the leaves. It's worth removing as many adults as you can on sunny spring days when they may be found basking on fritillary plants and young lily growth. Be quick – they'll drop to the ground and hide if they see you coming. If you have a big infestation to cope with, a white sheet or some paper spread beneath the plant may help.

Slugs and snails

There's no denying that some species of slugs and snails are among the chief villains of the pest world, destroying seedlings and making a real mess of mature plants. They are hard to catch in the daytime, but visit your seed bed on a damp night in summer and you may see armies of slugs chomping away, and perhaps a few snails too. Picking them off, on torchlight expeditions, works wonders, and that way you know you have caught some. But it isn't everyone's idea of a fun evening. Beer traps (plastic pots half-full of beer, sunk into the soil) are effective, but they can also drown beneficial insects such as ground beetles, which might

Codling moths

Codling moths

A healthy bird population helps greatly in controlling many kinds of caterpillar, but birds can't get at those of the damaging codling moth because they feed inside apples. A special pheromone trap (pictured), available from garden centres, is the best way to save your apple crop. The trap lures male codling moths to a sticky end and prevents breeding.

otherwise have been devouring slugs while you sleep. Upside-down grapefruit skins or squeezed-out lemon halves placed on the soil are a powerful slug attractant but you must regularly remove slugs hiding underneath them: after dark is the best time. Try to avoid slug pellets, which may be directly or indirectly damaging to natural slug and snail predators such as hedgehogs and thrushes. Other slug controls that you can buy include copper collars and tape, and biological predators in the form of parasitic nematodes, but both are quite expensive and must be used correctly to be effective.

Removing snails by hand is an eco-friendly tactic, and you can be sure that you've caught the culprits.

Copper collars are an expensive but quite effective slug deterrent. They work by reacting with the slug's slime to give it a slight electric shock.

Pesticides: the consequences

Chemical pesticides – even 'safer' organic alternatives such as pyrethrum – are nearly all non-specific, so they will destroy beneficial insects as well as those you are trying to control. There may be times, especially in the early stages of establishing a chemical-free garden, or in warm, dry weather in late spring, when you feel that aphids, for example, are getting the upper hand. But if you intervene to wipe them out, you risk not only killing beneficial insects such as hoverflies and ladybirds, which feed on aphids, but also depriving them of their natural food supply. It's much better (and less trouble) to be patient, so wipe or wash aphids or other insect pests off plants that are badly affected, and wait for the beneficial insects to arrive and do a neat clearing-up job for you.

The breaking down of dead or dying plant material to make fertile soil by recycling the organic matter it contains is a process that happens naturally wherever plants grow. In deciduous woodland leaves fall and rot down into humus, which conditions the soil. In the garden, you can harness this natural cycle by making compost. And if you manage your heap well, it can be a rich habitat for all kinds of wildlife.

Making compost

Try to site your compost area in a level part of the garden that is sunny for at least part of the day. To break down waste quickly, the heap needs to be warm, and making use of the sun's energy is a good way to start the process. Unless you have a huge garden with a great deal of waste to recycle, compost bins are easier to manage than heaps. They keep the compost tidier and retain heat and moisture more effectively. Many types of compost bin work well: timber structures can be bought in kit form or built from waste planks or pallets; alternatively, you can buy plastic or metal bins. Three bins make an ideal system: a mature one ready for use in the garden, one in the process of

When you start turning your garden and kitchen rubbish into compost, you'll probably be amazed at the volume of stuff a properly working heap will swallow up.

Don't forget

A warm, weatherproof compost heap can provide ideal living accommodation for a range of breeding or hibernating animals, from hedgehogs to slow-worms and from toads to mice and voles. It will be full of the creepy-crawlies they like to feed on. So be very cautious when you need to disturb your heap: you never know what you may find!

Compost-boosting plants

It may seem a bit odd to cultivate things specifically to cut them down and put them in the compost, but certain plants will boost the quality of your compost because they are especially efficient at gathering nutrients from the soil. Nettles are useful in this way (as well as being important for butterfly and moth caterpillars), and the composting plant that many organic gardeners wouldn't be without is comfrey (shown left). This plant has a deep tap root through which nutrients – especially potash, the element that promotes fruiting and flowering – are absorbed. The potash is stored in the leaves, so if you cut these and add them to your heap you'll have ideal compost for crops like tomatoes and soft fruit. Comfrey flowers are a great favourite with bees, too. Compost both nettles and comfrey before they set seed, or you could end up with too much of a good thing.

rotting down, and a third to put new waste in. Each bin needs a fitted lid or other rainproof cover that you can remove in showery weather if the contents get too dry. Large bins are more effective if you have the space: aim for a 1m (40in) cube.

The key to successful composting is a balanced mix of about three parts nitrogen-rich, live green waste, such as fresh lawn mowings and newly pulled weeds, to one part bulky carbon-rich material – dead leaves, torn-up cardboard, dry plant stalks and the like. Avoid the roots of perennial weeds, such as bindweed and ground elder, and unless your heap gets really hot, it may also be wise to exclude seeding weeds and any diseased plant

Soil organisms

Compost heaps are home to a secret army of little-known, normally invisible organisms that help the composting process. The populations of these tiny life-forms are staggering: a spoonful of compost can contain bacteria by the million, and nematodes and mites by the thousand, not to mention the fungi. Then there are worms, beetles, slugs, ants, woodlice, millipedes and other creatures big enough to recognize. These larger workers in the decomposition process include the shiny, dark reddish brandling worm, one of about ten common earthworm species found in gardens, and the one that is sometimes kept in wormeries for breaking down kitchen waste. Be thankful for the combined efforts of this battalion of unsung recyclers: without them we would be surrounded by heaps of dead plant material, instead of having lovely compost to enrich our gardens.

material. Coarse or woody material will take longer to rot down, so shred it before adding to the heap. A layer of twiggy material at the base of each heap is a good idea, as it helps with aeration and prevents waterlogging.

Compost heaps aren't just for garden waste. Quite a lot of what an average household throws away can be composted, from cardboard boxes and brown envelopes to coffee grounds and vegetable peelings. Don't include anything containing man-made materials such as plastics or polyester, which won't decompose, and don't add cooked food or meat, which may attract rats. But composting everything you can makes a huge amount of environmental sense, saving on transport and landfill and giving your garden soil a welcome boost of organic matter in the process.

There are compost bins to suit every garden and every household.

① Utility plastic compost bins work efficiently and are very easy to use.

② Reused tyres make an inexpensive and versatile solution.

③ A purpose-made container clad with trellis is a little more decorative.

Wormeries

A wormery produces small amounts of rich compost quickly and conveniently from kitchen waste, so it's ideal if you don't have space for a compost heap. Purpose-made wormery kits come with everything you need: brandling worms, bedding and a system of stacked bins that make it easy to feed the worms and collect the compost. There's also a tap for drawing off 'worm tea' – a rich liquid fertilizer.

A wormery is an ideal high-intensity composting system for a small space.

Plants for wildlife

One of the best things you can do to entice wildlife into your garden is to increase the variety of plants that you grow. A wide range of plants provides shelter and food for many creatures, great and small, at different seasons of the year. You'll be amazed by how soon new planting makes a difference, with birds arriving to investigate the exciting possibilities of new trees and shrubs, and bees and butterflies drawn to new sources of nectar. Oh, and you'll find your garden is a whole lot more interesting for humans, too.

Planting for biodiversity

'Biodiversity' is a relatively new word but it's a very important one. Sustaining a variety of different life forms is what it's all about and it is just as relevant whether you are talking about the planet or your garden. If you can increase the range of different plants and animals living in your garden, it will become a richer, healthier and more fascinating place.

Something for everyone: shrubs, flowers and water in this small area will attract all sorts of creatures.

All animal life depends, ultimately, on plants, in a variety of ways. Many garden creatures, from aphids and butterflies to snails and rabbits, eat nothing but plants. Others, including hoverflies, bats and sparrowhawks, are predators, living on plant-dependent insects or other animals. Some animals, such as frogs and many birds, normally depend on a mixture of plant and animal foods. Given that each animal has its own preferences, it's easy to see that gardens with lots of different plants are more likely to attract a broad spectrum of wildlife.

The role of gardens

People used to think that as a man-made, 'unnatural' habitat with many alien plants, gardens didn't really count as a serious resource for wildlife. But since the 1950s, wild plants and creatures have increasingly been squeezed out of the wider landscape. Built-up areas now stand where once there was woodland, wetland and pasture, and the use of weedkillers and insecticides has ensured that many once common plants and creatures are now rarities. And modern, monocultural farmland, where a single crop spreads over many acres, is useless to most forms of wildlife. On a more cheerful note, the value of gardens to wildlife is increasingly well understood and appreciated. Gardens typically contain a wide range of plants of many different types: trees, shrubs and climbers, fruit and vegetables, grass, hedges, perennial and annual flowers and, last but not least, weeds.

Native plants

The best wildlife gardens will include a proportion of native plants, and these needn't be difficult to integrate into a garden setting. Most people love cowslips and primroses, for example, and if you are choosing a tree such as a birch or a rowan, you may well find that the native silver birch (*Betula pendula*) and mountain ash (*Sorbus aucuparia*) are just as acceptable and attractive as their more 'refined' relatives from the Far East, which are less appealing to British insects. The wildlife value of a mixed hedge of suitable native plants (*see* pages 32–3) has been proven many times. But alongside the 'natives', don't underestimate the value of 'imports': buddleia isn't native but it's unquestionably a great plant for attracting butterflies; lavender is loved by bees; and hungry birds aren't fussy about where their seeds come from.

With all this in mind, you'll see that your garden's potential for attracting a diverse range of creatures is enormous, and it isn't difficult to turn that potential into a brilliant wildlife habitat – so don't wait any longer, get planting!

Trees

Field maple

Silver birch

Hazel

Hawthorn

One of the best ways to make your garden more attractive to wildlife is to plant a tree – or several, if there's space. A good tree can provide nectar, fruit and a resident insect population, and also places for birds to roost, perch, hide and nest. Native trees tend to be best for wildlife, though many, such as oak and ash, will outgrow most gardens. Here is a selection of trees for wildlife that won't get too big for an average-sized garden.

Field maple
Acer campestre

Britain's only native maple makes an attractive feature where there is space for a medium-sized tree. It supports a large insect population and is generous with its seed crop, which voles and wood mice enjoy. Field maples are especially successful on chalk and limestone soils. Their attractively shaped leaves turn a lovely rich gold in autumn.

Silver birch
Betula pendula

'The lady of the woods' is perhaps our most graceful native tree, whether clothed in spring green or autumn gold, or when the bare, fine twigs and infant catkins hang spangled with raindrops in winter. Its narrow shape, pale bark and open canopy create a light, airy effect, never casting heavy shade. Neither does it seem to take up a lot of garden space. Look out for self-sown seedlings to grow as replacements for mature trees: birch grows fast but is not a long-lived tree and may begin to fail after about 30 years.

Hazel
Corylus avellana

Though not a star performer, hazel can be an excellent choice if you have room for one or more large background shrubs or small trees. This native tree plays host to a good population of insects, and can be really useful if you cut it down to the ground every few years and let it regrow. That way it is easily kept to a manageable size, and as well as providing you with handy pea-sticks and poles, it helps create a good habitat for woodland wildflowers because the ground beneath won't be too shady. When fertilized by pollen blown from the catkins, the tiny, whiskery red spring flowers become hazelnuts.

Hawthorn
Crataegus

Most kinds of hawthorn make good garden trees. They put up with exposed sites and poor soil, and are fairly compact yet provide an abundant autumn berry crop for the birds. Their generous froth of blossom makes hawthorns a flagship feature of gardens and hedgerows in late spring, and most varieties also colour well in autumn. For wildlife, the native hawthorn (*Crataegus monogyna*) has the edge and is one of the best plants to include in a mixed hedge (*see* page 32). Midland hawthorn (*Crataegus laevigata*) is a less widespread native, better suited to heavy soils. Others include *Crataegus × lavalleei* 'Carrierei' and *Crataegus persimilis* 'Prunifolia'. Avoid the double-flowered types, some of which have pink blossom, as they generally don't bear fruit.

Apple and Crab apple
Malus

Apples and crabs alike have glorious, subtly scented spring blossom that attracts bees. They fruit plentifully when mature, providing a crop for you and windfalls for the birds. These may also bring in winter visitors such as fieldfares and redwings in hard weather, and resident blackbirds and thrushes appreciate them too. There are apple trees to suit everyone: dessert, cooker or crab apple, in sizes to suit any garden. For the smallest spaces, or for a container, find a tree grown on a dwarfing rootstock such as M116 or M27. If you decide to choose a crab apple, try the reliable *Malus hupehensis* or, for the best crab-apple jelly, *Malus* 'John Downie'. Older apple trees provide rich pickings for blue tits and other small birds that like to forage in bark crevices for aphids and other insects.

Cherry and Plum
Prunus

These ever-popular garden trees can be disease-prone, and the cultivated kinds with frilly, double flowers can be short on both nectar and fruit. Much better for wildlife is the simple, native wild cherry or gean (*Prunus avium*) or, for something more compact, try a wild

Trees for free

Most native trees produce a great many seeds, and those that are happy in your growing conditions may well reproduce very successfully. Learn to recognize the tiny self-sown seedlings of yew, birch, hazel, hawthorn and other species while you're weeding, and pot some up while they're small. Some will quickly make useful hedging plants or, in two or three years, home-grown native trees – rather special 'green' gifts for friends and family, or to donate to plant sales or local tree-planting schemes.

or cultivated plum (*Prunus domestica*) or the cherry plum (*Prunus cerasifera*, right), which provides a welcome touch of spring with pretty blossom very early in the year.

Rowan or Mountain ash
Sorbus

Excellent trees for gardens in town or country, most rowans are relatively compact and tolerate a wide range of soil types. They have spring flowers as well as colourful autumn fruits and leaves. The many species and cultivars differ in habit and berry colour (orange, red, pink or white), but all have ferny foliage that casts pleasant dappled shade. The native species *Sorbus aucuparia* is always popular with birds, while its narrow, upright cultivar 'Sheerwater Seedling' is useful for small gardens. Many other rowans are worth considering, including golden-berried *Sorbus* 'Joseph Rock', dainty, pink-fruited *Sorbus vilmorinii* and compact *Sorbus cashmiriana* with white berries.

Yew
Taxus baccata

Yew is one of our longest-lived trees, so plant it for posterity but also enjoy it now: it will grow faster than you think, and its dense foliage will soon provide snug winter cover and nesting places for your garden birds. The fleshy red berries on mature female trees provide a winter feast for blackbirds, thrushes, and visiting fieldfares and redwings. Yew can be pruned hard at any age, regenerating successfully even from very old wood. It's ideal for hedging and topiary, but it is highly toxic so don't plant it where livestock can reach it. Yew is happy in most conditions but not on soggy soil.

Apple

Cherry plum

Rowan

Yew

Shrubs and climbers

Buddleia

Shrubs and climbers help make a garden feel comfortable, dividing and furnishing the space and providing all-important structure. They are also invaluable wildlife plants, creating cover for feeding, nesting and security. From plants that suit your garden soil and situation, try to select those that will provide food for birds, mammals and insects at different seasons, so there is always something to attract wild visitors.

Buddleia
Buddleja

Either by accident or design, many gardens contain a buddleia. Although it self-sows rather freely, it is easy and quick to grow, and its nectar-rich flowers are a magnet for butterflies. A bush of it in full flower, covered with red admirals and painted ladies, is certainly a fine sight in mid- to late summer. It is also an important food plant for the larvae of many moths. You can prevent buddleias from becoming invasive by dead-heading before they set seed. And you'll get larger flowers and a less untidy bush if you hard prune every spring. The foliage can, however, be drab and flowering time is short, so if you're planting a new buddleia try 'Lochinch' (shown left), which has attractive, silvery foliage, and train a late-flowering clematis up through the branches to extend the season of interest.

Caryopteris

A compact flowering shrub with insect appeal, *Caryopteris* is useful in small spaces and makes a haze of blue in a sunny spot in late summer. It's best to cut it back to just a few inches high in spring so you can make space for bulbs and summer flowers before a new crop of neat grey foliage springs up. The shrub will go on to flower and produce a fresh delivery of nectar for the bees and butterflies, just as many other plants are fading.

Dogwoods and Cornelian cherry
Cornus

Most varieties of dogwood (*Cornus*) make good garden shrubs or trees. *Cornus alba* cultivars are grown for their coloured winter stems and their tolerance of damp soil. Those with variegated foliage look good all year: they include the vigorous *Cornus alba* 'Elegantissima', with bright red stems and cream-variegated foliage. Native *Cornus sanguinea*, common in chalk and limestone areas, also has garden cultivars with glowing winter stems: 'Midwinter Fire' and 'Winter Beauty' are the best known. *Cornus florida* and *Cornus kousa* are understandably fêted for their showy flowers (bracts). The Cornelian cherry (*Cornus mas*) is a large shrub or small tree, among the first on the scene in spring with its abundant, bobble-like, bright golden flowers. The big, juicy red fruits are loved by birds. For foliage interest as a bonus, try the prettily variegated form *Cornus mas* 'Variegata'.

Cotoneaster

From ground-hugging *Cotoneaster dammeri* to the vigorous, tree-like cultivar *Cotoneaster frigidus* 'Cornubia', most cotoneasters are good wildlife shrubs, even though they are not native plants. They are excellent for attracting birds and bees, and pleasing to look at for much of the year. *Cotoneaster horizontalis* is ideal

Caryopteris

Cornelian cherry

Cotoneaster

for a partly shaded wall where its twiggy branches will make good nesting cover, and where it will produce abundant berries for the blackbirds in midwinter. Bees just love the tiny pinkish flowers in late spring. To add extra wildlife value, plant a summer-flowering honeysuckle or clematis to scramble up through the cotoneaster's branches. It will provide nectar for moths and butterflies.

Spindle
Euonymus europaeus

An interesting deciduous shrub native to chalk and limestone areas, spindle will grow on any well-drained soil. It has remarkably exotic-looking fruits: their shocking-pink cases split open on the branches to reveal seeds of dazzling orange, from which it is quite easy to grow new plants. The leaves of many spindles colour well in autumn, especially those of the easily obtainable cultivar 'Red Cascade'. Other types of spindle include *Euonymus alatus*, which has deep-pink autumn leaves, and *Euonymus planipes*, a larger shrub/tree with correspondingly outsize fruits.

Common ivy
Hedera helix

If you allow ivy to get out of control it can easily become a weed, but don't let that blind you to its virtues as a wildlife plant. Autumn is the time when the mature plants attract bees to their valuable nectar-rich flowers, and now that ivy is fruiting more reliably it sustains birds, which in turn deposit the pink, pearly seeds that you sometimes find on lawns and paths. Keep ivy away from old walls with loose mortar and only allow it to climb up trees with dense canopies.

Their shade will help to control its spread, but make sure you restrict the ivy to the trunk of the tree, pruning it out of the branch canopy. For wildlife, it's best to propagate ivy from a mature plant because ivy does not flower when young. The cuttings can be grown as shrubs or trained on a fence to create an unusual evergreen hedge.

Sea buckthorn
Hippophae rhamnoides

This tough, thicket-forming shrub is native to dunes and scrubby areas near the sea. It is brilliant for coastal gardens, tolerating salt spray and gales, but there's no reason for seaside gardeners to keep it to themselves. Its thorny, silver-leaved stems quickly grow into a tall screen or shelter belt, giving good protection and nesting cover for birds. If you grow both male and female plants you can look forward to abundant crops of golden-orange berries, which last well into winter and sustain birds in hard weather.

Holly
Ilex aquifolium

Its glossy leaves and scarlet berries make holly one of the more uplifting evergreen shrubs. Whether you allow it to grow informally or clip it into shape, holly provides good cover and shelter for birds and insects. You will need a female variety to be sure of winter berries, and you may need to plant a male too, for pollination, if there isn't one near by – though the variety 'J.C. van Tol' is partly self-fertile. Birds have an irritating habit of ignoring holly berries until just before Christmas, so if you want to save some for decoration, tie a net bag over a branch or two to avoid disappointment.

Spindle

Ivy

Sea buckthorn

Holly

Himalayan honeysuckle

Honeysuckle

Firethorn

Rose

Himalayan honeysuckle
Leycesteria formosa

This distinctive, vigorous shrub from the Far East isn't a honeysuckle at all, but it's easy to grow and useful for forming rapid cover. The hanging bunches of white flowers have long-lasting deep-red bracts, and the green arching stems are attractive in winter. Birds are fond of the purple fruits – hence the shrub's other common name, pheasant berry.

Common honeysuckle
Lonicera periclymenum

With a little forethought, you can have honeysuckle in flower from late spring to autumn if you have room to plant several varieties. Reliable for scent are cultivars of the native wild honeysuckle *Lonicera periclymenum*. 'Belgica', flowering from late spring, and 'Serotina', lasting into autumn, are both pink and cream, while the excellent 'Graham Thomas' has cream flowers over a very long season. Honeysuckle makes a brilliant nectar bar for moths on warm summer nights including an exotic-looking deep-pink one, the elephant hawkmoth. It is named for the trunk-like snout of its remarkable-looking caterpillar, which feeds on rosebay and other willowherbs.

Firethorn
Pyracantha

Available with red, orange or yellow berries, pyracantha is a splendid shrub to train, espalier-style, against an east- or west-facing house wall. Clip the new growth back after flowering so you leave the flower trusses to mature into berries. These will enhance the appearance of your house all through the autumn as well as providing a winter fruit crop for blackbirds and thrushes. Pyracantha makes valuable sheltered nesting cover and can be grown as a hedge or a free-standing shrub – it makes a spiny, predator-proof thicket in a wild garden where there's plenty of space.

Rose
Rosa

Many simple single roses lend themselves to natural wildlife gardens. Choose a variety that follows up its flowers with a reliable crop of hips – good for winter interest in the garden and helpful to hungry birds in hard winter weather (though for many rose hips aren't their first choice). *Rosa glauca* (shown left) offers interesting greyish-pink foliage as well as flowers and hips; the sweet briar *Rosa rubiginosa* has fragrant foliage,

Brambles: the pros and cons

The mention of brambles may strike terror into the heart of some gardeners, particularly those faced with the back-breaking task of hacking out a garden plot or allotment from waste land overrun with this potentially invasive monster of a plant. If your garden is small, you'll doubtless prefer to do your blackberrying elsewhere, unless you grow one of the cultivated thornless forms such as 'Oregon Thornless' or 'Loch Ness' (shown left). But if you have plenty of ground to spare, your own sunny bramble patch will give you a lot of pleasure as you watch the bees, butterflies and other insects that are drawn to bramble flowers. Birds, too, will nest in its safe, thorny cover, and both you and your feathered friends can enjoy its juicy fruits in autumn.

smelling of apples. *Rosa rugosa*, which is available in both pink- and white-flowered forms, or one of its single-flowered cultivars, is a particularly good choice for a hedge; bare-root plants are usually available from late autumn. *Rosa rugosa* has healthy foliage, a robust constitution and tomato-like hips.

Rosemary
Rosmarinus officinalis

The pungent fragrance of this well-loved Mediterranean herb seems to capture the essence of summer even on miserable winter days. Give it a warm, sunny spot (it will tolerate the poorest soil provided it isn't wet) and rosemary will reward you with blue flowers before most of the garden wakes up in spring – a great standby for early bees. With age, the bushes acquire a woody skeleton that provides lots of sheltered nooks and crannies for overwintering insects. There are varieties of rosemary to suit whatever garden space you have available, from 'Miss Jessopp's Upright' (purple-blue flowers) to the much lower-growing 'Severn Sea' and the creeping (but less hardy) varieties of the Prostratus Group.

Butcher's broom
Ruscus aculeatus

This spiky little native evergreen shrub is quite shade-tolerant, covering the ground beneath garden trees just as it does in wild woodland. Its star turn is its display of big, long-lasting, globular red berries, which usually last all winter long. The fruits are freely produced where the shade is not too deep. You will need to grow both male and female plants to get berries, unless you can get hold of the hermaphrodite form.

Elder
Sambucus nigra

Wild elder makes an ungainly shrub if left unpruned, although birds will enjoy its berries just the same. Why not choose one of several cultivars that have ornamental leaves as well as berries? *Sambucus nigra* 'Gerda' has deep-purple foliage, 'Aurea' has golden foliage, and there are elders with delicately cut leaves such as *Sambucus nigra* f. *laciniata* (green) or 'Eva' (purple again, shown right). All have the familiar, headily scented early summer blossom that is good for making elderflower cordial – you don't need many flowerheads. Keep elders manageable by pruning them in winter: either take out a few of the oldest branches each year, or cut the whole thing down to a stump every few years, in which case you will lose a year's blossom and the birds a year's fruit.

Viburnum

In the viburnum species you'll find a wide range of tough and useful garden shrubs, from the evergreen laurustinus (*Viburnum tinus*) offering dense cover and winter nectar, to the native guelder rose (*Viburnum opulus*, shown right), a deciduous shrub with delicate lacecap spring blossom and bunches of glossy red berries. These fruits look wonderful and they give the garden welcome colour all winter, but birds tend to leave them until last. They are, however, good standby rations if really cold weather makes blackbirds, thrushes and winter visitors such as fieldfares desperate enough to eat them when other fruit has run out. Provided you plant both the male and female forms, another viburnum, the low-growing evergreen *Viburnum davidii*, will produce amazing turquoise berries.

Rosemary

Butcher's broom

Purple-leaved elder

Viburnum

Berries and fruit

There's a huge range of fruiting plants, large and small, with berries in almost every colour you can think of. Most have fruits that ripen in autumn, ready to cheer the garden when flowers are becoming scarcer, and to sustain fruit-eating birds and small mammals through the lean months of the year. An area planted with berrying trees and shrubs will keep the supply lines going (*see* opposite).

The golden-berried rowan, *Sorbus* 'Joseph Rock', is popular with both gardeners and blackbirds for its reliably abundant berry crop.

Birds and berries

Berrying plants and fruit-eating birds have a mutually beneficial relationship. Blackbirds and thrushes, in particular, relish the fruits of many common garden plants, from berberis and pyracantha to currants and apples. The plants benefit by having their seeds dispersed (accompanied by a boosting dollop of fertilizer) when a bird digests the fruit's flesh and passes the pip or seed in its droppings. When you're weeding and you come upon chance seedlings of hawthorn, ivy, cotoneaster and mahonia, it's usually because a plant has successfully reproduced itself by this method.

Birds are not equally interested in all berries, which is an advantage. If you plant only the birds' favourites, the garden will be stripped of much of its potential winter colour by late autumn, so plan for at least some berries that won't have vanished by Christmas. Skimmia, *Aucuba* and guelder rose (*Viburnum opulus*) tend to be left when other berries have been gobbled up. In a mild winter some berries may stay on their branches until spring, but in late-winter snow the less popular ones may come into their own as life-saving rations. Ivy berries, which ripen much later than others, are hugely valuable to birds in the chilly days of early spring when food can be really scarce. Windfall apples and crab apples are well received in winter, and if you have somewhere to store a few freshly picked apples in the autumn they make good emergency fare in cold weather, and may bring fieldfares and redwings into your garden when there's snow.

Sharing your fruit

If you're feeling extra-generous, you might even consider sharing your soft fruit crop. Blackbirds love redcurrants and ripe gooseberries, and a laden bush or two may have a large enough crop for you to leave some unpicked, for them to enjoy as a treat. Wild or alpine strawberries are also a good wildlife standby. These easy and shade-tolerant little plants can be tucked in under shrubs to provide useful ground cover and a long season of small, sweet fruits for whoever gets to pick them first.

Rosa 'Geranium' is a fine, multi-season rose with delicate foliage and single, blood-red flowers, followed by these shapely hips, which birds rather like.

Don't forget

Fruiting wall shrubs such as pyracantha and flowering quince need to be pruned after flowering each year to keep them close to the wall. You'll sacrifice some infant berries, but the rest will ripen better and the shrub will look more attractive if it doesn't outgrow its space.

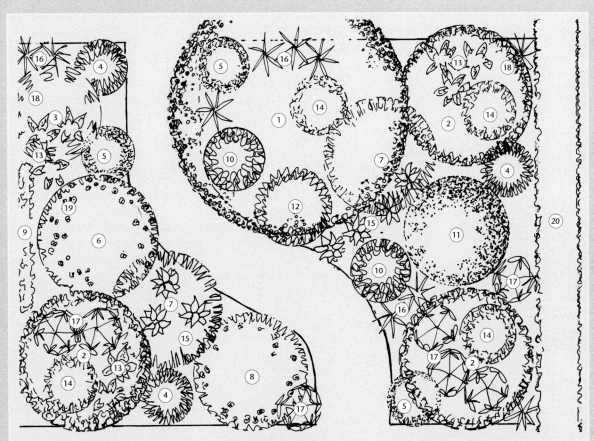

Tree

1 Rowan (*Sorbus aucuparia*) (x 1)

Shrubs and climbers

2 Hazel (*Corylus avellana*) (x 3)

3 Purple cut-leaved elder (*Sambucus nigra* 'Eva') (x 1)

4 Butcher's broom (*Ruscus aculeatus*) (x 3)

5 *Berberis thunbergii* f. *atropurpurea* 'Atropurpurea Nana' (x 3)

6 *Rosa* 'Geranium' (x 1)

7 *Cornus alba* 'Sibirica Variegata' (x 2)

8 Guelder rose (*Viburnum opulus* 'Compactum') (x 1)

9 Honeysuckle (*Lonicera periclymenum* 'Belgica'; trained on fence) (x 1)

10 Spurge laurel (*Daphne laureola*) (x 2)

11 *Cotoneaster conspicuus* (x 1)

12 *Hedera helix* 'Arborescens' (x 1)

Perennials

13 Marbled arum (*Arum italicum* subsp. *italicum* 'Marmoratum') (x 8)

14 Sweet woodruff (*Galium odoratum*) (x 4)

15 *Pulmonaria rubra* (x 7)

16 Stinking iris (*Iris foetidissima*) (x 8)

17 Stinking hellebore (*Helleborus foetidus*) (x 7)

Bulbs

18 Snowdrop (*Galanthus nivalis*) (x 100)

19 *Narcissus* 'Jenny' (x 50)

20 Mixed hedge: hawthorn, holly, spindle, yew, blackthorn (2 of each)

Berries in season

Summer: Bird cherry (*Prunus avium*), wild and cultivated cherries, mahonia, redcurrants, wild strawberry

Early autumn: *Amelanchier*, apples and crab apples, arum, berberis, blackberries, elder, hawthorn, honeysuckle, plums, rowan, sea buckthorn, spindle

Late autumn: Blackthorn, buckthorn, holly, rose hips, yew

Early winter: cotoneaster, mistletoe, myrtle, pyracantha, snowberry

Late winter: Ivy

A WOODLAND AREA WITH BERRYING PLANTS FOR BIRDS
7.5 x 5M (25 x 16FT)

The plan above is filled with plants to attract wildlife and forms part of a long, narrow garden, spanning its width. Coppiced hazel creates a woodland effect, with all-year interest as you walk through it from one part of the garden to another. For autumn and winter colour there is a variety of berries – on shrubs and a rowan tree, on the hedging plants and, at ground level, on irises and marbled arums.

Border flowers

A well-planned flower bed with a carefully chosen mix of plants can be a haven for all kinds of wildlife, providing nectar and pollen for insects almost all year round, seeds for birds, and places for creatures from spiders to hedgehogs to shelter and forage. Remember to delay clearing away at least some of last year's stems and seedheads until the spring; this will markedly increase your border's value to wildlife in winter.

Achillea

Agastache

Allium

Columbine

Achillea

Common yarrow (*Achillea millefolium*) is a familiar and tough lawn weed or meadow flower (depending on your point of view), with flat plates of tiny white flowers that are excellent for insects. Yarrow's more flamboyant relatives make better border plants, though, with a wide colour range and plenty of insect appeal when in flower. The attractive seedheads that follow provide shelter for small spiders and insects well into autumn. Choose the old, bright yellow favourites 'Coronation Gold' or 'Gold Plate', or for a change of colour try the aptly named deep-red 'Summerwine' or orange 'Terracotta' (shown left). The garden forms of *Achillea* are fairly tolerant, but they won't flourish in clay soil that is very poorly drained.

Agastache

Attractive to bees and butterflies and tolerant of dry soils, anise hyssop (*Agastache rugosa*, shown left) has been around in herb gardens for a long time and has recently helped spawn quite a few cultivars that have become rather fashionable plants. *Agastache* 'Blue Fortune' is among the best of the traditional blue/purple forms; *Agastache rugosa* 'Golden Jubilee' has golden leaves, and there are other new arrivals with orange, pink or white flowers. The foliage is aromatic, smelling of mint or liquorice.

Allium

Bees love the flowers of most onions and their relatives. Many 'ornamental' varieties such as the chic *Allium schubertii* and the striking *Allium cristophii* (shown left) also have architectural seedheads that last well into autumn. Even stray leeks or garlic, left in a corner of the vegetable patch, will throw up attractive globular flowerheads in their second year. If you grow several types of allium – with overlapping flowering seasons – you will certainly keep bees happy for months. Common chives (*Allium schoenoprasum*) and the taller garlic or Chinese chives (*Allium tuberosum*), flowering in spring and late summer respectively, are also great herbs for the kitchen. The beguiling three-cornered leek (*Allium triquetrum*) blooms early with white bell-shaped flowers, but you need to keep an eye on it as the small bulblets soon become invasive. *Allium hollandicum* has purple globes on tall stems in late spring, while *Allium sphaerocephalon* is great for brightening up a late-summer border with its oval, wine-red flowerheads.

Columbine
Aquilegia

There are many refined garden aquilegias, all relatives or cultivars of the wild columbine *Aquilegia vulgaris*, but the ordinary cottage-garden 'mongrels', often called 'granny's bonnets', are hard to beat. Attractive, scalloped foliage appears in early spring followed by exquisitely formed flowers in shades of blue, purple, pink and white. Columbines scatter their seed about generously, especially on chalky or other lime-rich soils, but as they flower long before other border plants need the space, chance seedlings are usually welcome.

Michaelmas daisy
Aster

These are key plants for keeping borders colourful and well stocked with nectar, right into autumn. The best Michaelmas daisies to choose with wildlife in mind are tried-and-tested cultivars with a long flowering season, such as *Aster* 'Little Carlow' and *Aster × frikartii* 'Mönch'. Certain varieties are more effective than others at attracting butterflies, for example *Aster amellus* 'King George'. *Aster lateriflorus* var. *horizontalis* has masses of tiny daisies that change colour as they age, borne on a stiff, wiry plant that stands well into winter.

Perennial cornflower
Centaurea montana

Putting up with drought and neglect, this cottage-garden stalwart is among the first herbaceous plants to flower, providing not only nectar for spring insects but also welcome splashes of purplish blue in early garden borders. Cut it down after flowering and it will perform again in late summer and autumn, eventually helping to sustain seed-eating finches in winter with its hard, bristly seedheads. These are similar to those of the related grassland wildflowers, greater and common knapweed.

Red valerian
Centranthus ruber

Often associated with the seaside, red valerian will flower from late spring to autumn and is a reliable nectar plant – a particular favourite with a remarkable day-flying moth, the hummingbird hawkmoth (*see* page 101). It's a good idea to cut the plant down after its first flowering. This will encourage it to flower again as well as preventing it from seeding too freely. Red valerian resists drought and wind well, and will grow in almost any sunny spot. Be careful, though, not to let the plant seed into structural walls where its expanding fleshy roots can loosen mortar.

Teasel
Dipsacus fullonum

You can sum up the main reason for growing teasels in a single word: goldfinches. These delightful, colourful little birds (*see* page 87) are attracted to this self-sowing, prickly biennial like no other plant, tugging out the seeds as a winter treat. Teasel flowers open in early summer, starting as a lavender stripe around the middle of the spiny cone at the head of each stem and spreading, rather curiously, both up and down the cone at the same time to make two parallel bands of open flowers. They are full of nectar, attracting bees, butterflies and hoverflies. The stiff, structural skeletons of teasels stand up well to winter weather, looking charming when covered with hoar frost or snow (or, for that matter, when draped with dew-laden cobwebs in early autumn). A word of warning: pull up any unwanted self-sown seedlings while they are still tiny. Prickles and a tenacious tap root make this a tricky job once the plants are established.

Michaelmas daisy

Perennial cornflower

Red valerian

Teasel

Coneflower
Echinacea purpurea

A garden border 'must' for late summer and suitable for all but the very driest soil, echinaceas offer abundant nectar and the plants look appealing both when they are in bloom and, later, when seedheads form. A long season of flowers after many herbaceous plants are over ensures visits from butterflies such as red admirals, which are often at their most abundant in late summer. Echinaceas are prairie plants and combine well with grasses.

Eryngium

The true sea holly (*Eryngium maritimum*) grows wild on sandy and shingly coasts, but you are more likely to see its relatives in gardens. Many are perennial, but one of the most familiar is the biennial *Eryngium giganteum,* Miss Willmott's ghost (shown left). Striking, thistle-like flowers provide copious midsummer nectar for bees and hoverflies and are followed by nutritious seeds for finches in autumn, when they are also often hung with spiders' webs that sparkle with droplets of moisture. The plant's statuesque, spiny skeleton is famously photogenic when covered in frost and snow, though it tends to disintegrate by early winter in wet seasons. Look out for self-sown seedlings.

Eupatorium

Wild hemp agrimony (*Eupatorium cannabinum*) scarcely earns its space in gardens, with its rather wishy-washy greyish-pink flowers and its tendency to seed everywhere. But the garden forms of *Eupatorium maculatum* (known in the USA as Joe Pye weed) also attract insects and have the bonus of more richly coloured flowers. Some forms have rich purple stems as well, making the plant a more valuable border feature while you're waiting for it to flower: *Eupatorium maculatum* Atropurpureum Group 'Riesenschirm' (shown left) is a tried-and-tested variety. Leave the fluffy seedheads intact so that they shimmer in low winter light; the hollow stems also provide shelter for overwintering insects.

Fennel
Foeniculum vulgare

Both the green- and bronze-leaved forms of this kitchen herb are great wildlife plants, appealing particularly to hoverflies, those valuable aphid predators. The feathery young foliage of fennel makes good company for spring bulbs and other early flowers, and the architectural stems and seedheads last for months after the flowers are over. You can either cut down the stems before the seeds ripen or leave them for the birds in winter – obviously the more wildlife-friendly option, as long as you weed out unwanted seedlings while still small enough to pull out easily. As a reward, you will enjoy the skeletons in autumn and winter, when they look wonderful draped with cobwebs or rimed with frost.

Catmint
Nepeta

Catmints can be a mixed blessing. They are easy to grow and drought-tolerant, and they provide nectar, shelter and a long season of flowers – all very welcome attributes in a wildlife garden. Unfortunately they also hold a magnetic attraction for cats, which you'll probably prefer to keep away from your garden birds. A home-made dome of wire-

Coneflower

Eryngium

Eupatorium

Fennel

netting bent over the crown of the plant makes it more inaccessible to cats and may prevent them from rolling in it. And if cats aren't a problem you will find catmint a first-rate nectar plant, bringing in bees, butterflies and moths including the silver Y – named for the white mark in the shape of a letter Y on its wings.

Lungwort
Pulmonaria

Flowering from late winter through to spring, the various species and cultivars of this shade-loving, cottage-garden favourite certainly earn their keep. The blue, pink or white flowers supply energy-boosting nectar for early bees, and the ground-covering leaves are often attractively spotted and silvered. *Pulmonaria rubra*, with coral flowers, is usually the earliest in bloom, followed by many blue-flowered forms of which the best include 'Lewis Palmer' (deep-blue flowers, vividly spotted leaves) and 'Blue Ensign', with plain leaves. If the first crop of foliage gets mildew by early summer, cut it off and the plant will grow fresh, disease-free leaves.

Ice plant
Sedum spectabile

The true ice plant and its white-flowered form *Sedum spectabile* 'Iceberg' are top-flight butterfly plants, flowering at the height of the butterfly season in late summer and autumn. Like most nectar plants, they work best in sunny places. A lot of hybrid sedums are also on sale, many of them beefier, brighter and more robust than *Sedum spectabile*, but the butterflies often seem unimpressed. Bees tend to be less choosy, and are happy with most sedums, such as the stalwart

Sedum 'Herbstfreude' (Autumn Joy), which has especially long-lasting seedheads that often sail through until early spring. Avoid rich, damp soil: the plants grow too lush and floppy, and stand up less well to cold, wet weather.

Mullein
Verbascum

There are several species of mullein and a great many more cultivars. Many kinds are very attractive to hoverflies and look good in a border. Most are biennials or short-lived perennials, but they all hybridize freely and set large amounts of seed. One of the best perennial mulleins is *Verbascum chaixii* 'Album', with purple-eyed white flowers on tall, slender spikes. Great mullein (*Verbascum thapsus*) is a biennial with attractive overwintering leaf rosettes and yellow or creamy-white flowers. Its mature leaves attract the caterpillars of the mullein moth – a test for the wildlife gardener!

Verbena
Verbena bonariensis

There's every reason why *Verbena bonariensis* has become a must-have plant: it keeps on flowering when many other herbaceous plants are over, and it takes up little space, holding its flowers on stiff, tall stems high above other border plants. It is also irresistible to many bees and to the exquisite butterflies of late summer, such as painted ladies and red admirals. As a South American native (*bonariensis* means from Buenos Aires), the verbena may struggle in colder gardens; an alternative here is its relative, the old-fashioned herb vervain (*Verbena officinalis*), a much less showy plant but even more popular with bees.

Lungwort

Ice plant

Mullein

Verbena

Nectar plants

Nectar is a very effective lure to the insects that pollinate flowering plants so they can reproduce successfully. Bees and butterflies, especially, are irresistibly drawn to this liquid mix of natural sugars, which serves as an energy-boosting life-saver when these creatures emerge from hibernation on sunny days in late winter. Fortunately, a huge number of our favourite garden plants are rich in nectar, so a flower border planted with insects in mind will almost certainly please us, too (*see* opposite).

So, what makes a good nectar plant? Well, it has nothing to do with the splendour of the flowers. Double flowers and those of many other intensively bred plants tend to have little to offer visiting insects. Modern plant breeding has tended to value big, showy flowers more highly than the welfare of the insect world, so the latest double begonia or frilly carnation is unlikely to attract non-human admirers. Many good nectar plants, including garden herbs, have rather inconspicuous flowers, and generally the simpler, old-fashioned flower forms are the best ones to choose for nectar-feeding insects. That doesn't mean they have to be drab, though: foxgloves, hellebores, wallflowers, red valerian, ice plant and *Verbena bonariensis* all produce plentiful nectar, as do many winter-flowering heathers. Flower shape doesn't seem to affect the amount of nectar, though it does determine which insects can gain access to it (*see* page 102).

Unusual nectar plants

The next time you visit somewhere flowery on a sunny day – be it a garden centre or a country lane – note the plants that are attracting bees and

Borage is a fast-growing annual for light soils, with beautiful blue flowers that are good for bees (and in summer drinks).

Ten nectar-rich garden herbs

Herb gardens are usually alive with bees and most herbs fit into a wildlife garden very well. Here are some to try:

Chives (*Allium schoenoprasum*)
Borage (*Borago officinalis*)
Fennel (*Foeniculum vulgare*)
Hyssop (*Hyssopus officinalis*)
Spearmint (*Mentha spicata*)
Wild marjoram (*Origanum vulgare*)
Rosemary (*Rosmarinus officinalis*)
Sage (*Salvia officinalis*)
Summer savory (*Satureja hortensis*)
Thyme (*Thymus vulgaris*)

butterflies. There will probably be many, and they may give you some new ideas for the garden. A number of quite unusual garden shrubs, such as *Clerodendrum bungei*, *Escallonia bifida* and *Hoheria sexstylosa*, are powerfully attractive to bees. *Calamintha nepeta*, *Veronicastrum* and gayfeather (*Liatris spicata*) are examples of less well-known herbaceous perennials with flowers that are rich in nectar.

Coneflower (*Echinacea purpurea*) is great with other plants in a nectar border, producing good seedheads as a bonus at the end of its long flowering season.

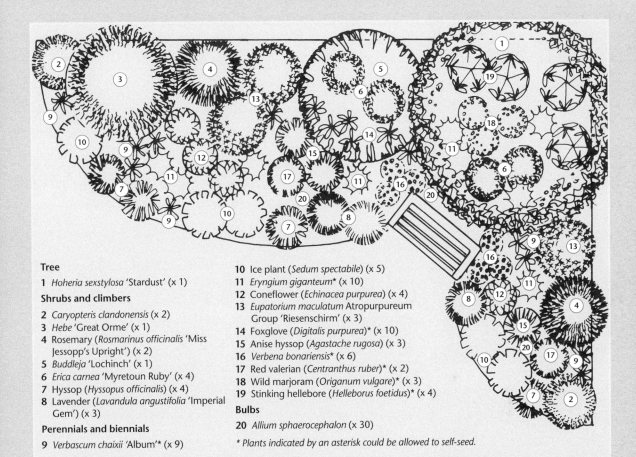

Tree

1 *Hoheria sexstylosa* 'Stardust' (x 1)

Shrubs and climbers

2 *Caryopteris clandonensis* (x 2)
3 *Hebe* 'Great Orme' (x 1)
4 Rosemary (*Rosmarinus officinalis* 'Miss Jessopp's Upright') (x 2)
5 *Buddleja* 'Lochinch' (x 1)
6 *Erica carnea* 'Myretoun Ruby' (x 4)
7 Hyssop (*Hyssopus officinalis*) (x 4)
8 Lavender (*Lavandula angustifolia* 'Imperial Gem') (x 3)

Perennials and biennials

9 *Verbascum chaixii* 'Album'* (x 9)

10 Ice plant (*Sedum spectabile*) (x 5)
11 *Eryngium giganteum** (x 10)
12 Coneflower (*Echinacea purpurea*) (x 4)
13 *Eupatorium maculatum* Atropurpureum Group 'Riesenschirm' (x 3)
14 Foxglove (*Digitalis purpurea*)* (x 10)
15 Anise hyssop (*Agastache rugosa*) (x 3)
16 *Verbena bonariensis** (x 6)
17 Red valerian (*Centranthus ruber*)* (x 2)
18 Wild marjoram (*Origanum vulgare*)* (x 3)
19 Stinking hellebore (*Helleborus foetidus*)* (x 4)

Bulbs

20 *Allium sphaerocephalon* (x 30)

* Plants indicated by an asterisk could be allowed to self-seed.

A NECTAR-RICH SUMMER BORDER TO ENCOURAGE BUTTERFLIES AND BEES
7.5 x 5M (25 x 16FT)

A sunny corner out of the wind is always a good spot for a garden seat, especially with the relaxing background hum of bees, and butterflies and other insects to watch. The nectar-rich, sun-loving plants in this border span much of the year, reaching a summer peak when the unusual evergreen shrub or small tree *Hoheria sexstylosa* 'Stardust' opens its intoxicating, honey-scented flowers.

When choosing nectar plants, don't forget moths. Some adult moths don't feed at all, but many (though not all) of those that do tend to fly and feed at night. Providing for them is no hardship, because most good moth plants are wonderfully fragrant. They include honeysuckle, jasmine, evening primrose, night-scented stock and sweet rocket (*Hesperis matronalis*).

Nectar plants are much more likely to attract insects if they are in a sunny, sheltered position. Make sure your nectar border doesn't get too dry in hot weather, though: water is needed for the nectar production process, and well-watered plants can produce more of it. Include plants that will yield nectar over a long season, from early spring (*see* Nectar plants for early spring on page 117) to late autumn, when queen bees and some butterflies are preparing to hibernate and need to build up their reserves in readiness. Good nectar plants for autumn include mature ivy, some Michaelmas daisies, sedums and red valerian.

Don't forget

Insects sometimes 'cheat' by piercing the base of the flower to get at the nectar more easily, without having to go the long way round. This means they don't collect and redistribute pollen and, as a result, the flowers remain unfertilized. If your runner beans haven't set, it's worth examining the flowers for damage, to find out if 'nectar piracy' is the cause!

Grassland plants

Cuckoo flower

Wild carrot

Snakeshead fritillary

Ox-eye daisy

Britain's grasslands, from damp meadows to dry downland, were traditionally among our very richest wildlife habitats – open and sunny, and with a wide range of plants to entice butterflies, bees and many other insects. Sadly, owing to drainage and building schemes, changing farming practices or simple neglect over the last 50 years or so, almost all of these grasslands have disappeared. It can be tricky to get the balance of plants right when you try to create flowery grassland in your garden (*see* pages 40–1), but if you succeed it can be hugely rewarding. There are many more wildflowers that can be grown successfully in grass, so be prepared to experiment.

Cuckoo flower
Cardamine pratensis

Also known as lady's smock, this delicate spring flower's native habitat – damp meadowland – is often lost when land is drained. It does, however, naturalize well in damp, grassy areas and is one of the plants that may materialize if you stop mowing a damp lawn. It is an important food plant for both the orange tip and the green-veined white butterflies: look carefully and you may find the distinctive orange eggs of the former stuck to the stems beneath the flower buds.

Wild carrot
Daucus carota

Often found growing wild on chalk downs, cliff tops and other dry grassland, wild carrot is very attractive to insects when in flower. Its foliage gives off a carrot-like scent when crushed. After flowering, the plant produces intricate semi-enclosed, cage-like seedheads, hence one of its common names, 'bird's nest'. The seedheads provide visual interest in the garden as well as winter seeds for birds, and they also offer nooks and crannies to shelter small insects.

Snakeshead fritillary
Fritillaria meleagris

Water meadows – damp riverside fields that were allowed to flood in winter – were the classic habitat for this exquisite little spring flower. As well as the distinctive mauve-coloured chequered variety, there is also a white-petalled form. It is surprisingly easy to grow from bought bulbs: plant them in grass that doesn't dry out too easily but avoid areas that are poorly drained with ground that stays soggy. If you're lucky, the plants will seed and you'll eventually have your own little fritillary meadow.

Ox-eye daisy
Leucanthemum vulgare

Capturing the essence of early summer, their shining white discs swaying in the grass, ox-eye or moon daisies soon colonize dry banks and verges near new roads, and are equally obliging in the garden. The plants do tend to run out of steam after a few years, but by then they will probably have seeded themselves and you won't be short of replacements. Vetches, poppies and any flowering grasses make good companions.

Ragged robin
Lychnis flos-cuculi

These days the damp pastures where this fragile-looking wildflower used to grow have mostly been drained, leaving it few strongholds in the wild. But ragged robin is tougher than it appears and adapts well to gardens, looking lovely growing with meadowsweet in the grass near a pond, or in a damp lawn in a sunny or partially shaded spot. It self-seeds readily and may well become naturalized.

Cowslip
Primula veris

Once a very common wildflower of unimproved grassland, this old-fashioned favourite is a good 'starter' plant for a new meadow area. It is not usually hard to establish in dryish, sunny, grassy spots, especially on chalky or other lime-rich soils. The spring flowers are a good source of nectar for bees. If cowslips like your patch of garden they will seed generously: delay cutting the grass around them until after midsummer, to

allow them to ripen and shed their seed. Young self-sown plants are easily moved to begin new colonies (or potted up and given to friends to convert them to the wildflower habit). Cowslip clumps can also be split into a number of rosettes, each of which will make a new plant.

Yellow rattle
Rhinanthus minor

The meadow-maker's friend, yellow rattle is a native annual worth including in seed mixtures for flowering meadows on all but the poorest soil. Its semi-parasitic roots will suck nutrients from those of various grasses, curbing their tendency to overwhelm less robust meadow flowers. You will probably have to go to a wildflower specialist to obtain seeds of yellow rattle. These do not store well but if you can get a few plants going you can collect your own seeds (they're ripe when the seedheads rattle, hence the name). Scatter them generously each year while they are still fresh, and you'll soon have enough plants to pass seed on to meadow-making friends and neighbours.

Common valerian
Valeriana officinalis

With its stiff, tall stems and flat heads of tiny flowers, this robust, pretty wildflower resembles a pale pink verbena. A native plant of damp ground, it is wonderful for naturalizing, holds its own among grass and really deserves to be better known. Its appeal to garden wildlife lies in the early-summer flowers that last for many weeks and attract numerous insects, followed by seedheads that birds such as finches enjoy. Valerian can be grown from seed or planted as plugs, and mature plants can be split when dormant.

Ragged robin

Cowslip

Yellow rattle

Common valerian

The right grasses

Tough, vigorous, well-fed grasses may be what you need for a frequently mown lawn, or for a family garden that doubles as a football pitch. But such grasses are the sworn enemy of meadow flowers, which will soon give up the struggle to compete. If you are starting a meadow from scratch and can choose the grasses it contains, avoid robustly aggressive lawn species like perennial rye-grass (*Lolium perenne*) and cocksfoot (*Dactylis glomerata*). Your soil and light conditions will dictate which of the many possible finer grasses are suitable for your particular patch, but a few good ones to try are browntop bent (*Agrostis capillaris*), the smaller fescues (*Festuca*) and crested dog's tail (*Cynosurus cristatus*). Also worth including is sweet vernal grass (*Anthoxanthum odoratum*), the plant that gives that wonderful scent to new-mown hay.

Plants for seed

Most plants produce enough seed to reproduce themselves in abundance, and an average garden will produce many millions of seeds every year from its collection of trees and shrubs, plants in beds and borders, weeds and grasses. Try to include as many seed-rich plants as you can (*see* opposite) and you'll have plenty of customers ready and waiting to take advantage of this bountiful and incredibly varied harvest.

Birds and seeds

Seeds are very nutritious for birds as they contain both protein and fat. Commercial seed mixes are a familiar and effective way of attracting birds to a garden, and are a valuable supplement to natural foods, but be aware that many of the ingredients are imported. It's easy to forget that wild birds will relish seeds from plants you grow in your garden, the only 'food miles' being those flown by the birds to collect them. The stout beaks of finches and sparrows, for example, are specially adapted to extracting or cracking larger seeds, such as sunflower and thistle, while dunnocks, tits, robins, wrens and other small birds will eat a great variety of tiny seeds as part of a mixed diet.

The dead seedheads of numerous garden plants, and of wildflowers such as knapweeds, thistles and scabious, are a valuable food resource. Herbs such as sage, lemon balm and marjoram produce a useful seed crop, too, as do grasses and many common weeds such as shepherd's purse, hawkweeds and self-heal. And don't despise dandelions! Their 'clocks' are

Goldfinches have perfected the art of extracting seeds from intricate seedheads, such as this evening primrose.

Grow seed from seed

Many easy annuals and biennials quickly mature to produce seeds that are nutritious and delicious for birds. These are especially welcome in winter when natural food is scarce. Choose seed-producing plants that you can grow in an ordinary flower bed or vegetable plot: sunflowers, cornflowers, evening primrose, flax, pot marigolds and rudbeckias, for example. Avoid anything with double flowers, and any highly bred plants including F1 hybrids. Enjoy the flowers, then collect the ripe seeds to dry and store for the winter bird table.

the first seedheads of the year in most gardens, maturing very quickly in spring when all last year's seeds have disappeared – just at the time when goldfinch parents are feeding their young and need a boost.

In autumn, if you have plenty of architectural seedheads such as teasels and *Phlomis*, cut some and push the stems into heavy pots of earth or stones so they are held securely. Then position the pots outside the windows to give you a grandstand view of goldfinches and other birds that come

Seedheads of perennials and grasses really come into their own in autumn, glowing in low sunlight and helping birds to refuel for the long winter ahead.

1 Globe thistle (*Echinops ritro* 'Veitch's Blue') (x 2)

2 *Clematis tangutica* (trained on fence or trellis) (x 1)

3 Sunflower (*Helianthus annuus*) (x 5)

4 Bronze fennel (*Foeniculum vulgare* 'Purpureum')* (x 3)

5 *Phlomis russeliana* (x 5)

6 Teasel (*Dipsacus fullonum*)* (x 5)

7 *Salvia* × *superba* (x 8)

8 *Rudbeckia fulgida* var. *sullivantii* 'Goldsturm' (x 3)

9 *Eryngium giganteum** (x 5)

10 Blue flax (*Linum perenne*) (x 5)

11 *Achillea* 'Walther Funcke' (x 8)

12 Love-in-a-mist (*Nigella damascena*)* (white, sown in drifts)

13 Quaking grass (*Briza media*)* (x 5)

14 Pasque flower (*Pulsatilla vulgaris*) (x 8)

15 *Veronica umbrosa* 'Georgia Blue' (x 3)

16 *Ophiopogon planiscapus* 'Nigrescens' (x 8)

17 *Chionodoxa sardensis** (x 100) (along edges of path)

* Plants indicated by an asterisk could be allowed to self-seed.

A FRONT GARDEN RICH IN SEED PLANTS TO ATTRACT BIRDS 7.5 x 3M (25 x 10FT)

Front gardens are in the spotlight all year. In this plan, summer colour contrasts shades of blue with vibrant, warm colours. Later, the different seedheads of globe thistle, fennel, teasel, *Phlomis* and *Achillea*, together with the birds they attract, bring life to the garden through autumn and winter.

to feed on them in winter. They make an attractive feature, and even when the heads have been emptied of their seeds, birds may still visit in the hope of finding small insects sheltering inside the intricate structures.

Tree seeds

In the wild, especially in woodland, many trees produce an abundant seed harvest which provides valuable food for birds. This is something to bear in mind if you're choosing trees, especially for a larger garden. Acorns are a favourite of jays, while beech mast provides valuable winter sustenance for chaffinches and bramblings and also nuthatches, whose dagger-like beaks can cope with acorns and hazelnuts, too. Conifer seeds, including those of pine and spruce, are popular with sharp-billed birds such as treecreepers and coal tits, as well as siskins, and in winter the tiny seeds of birch and alder sometimes bring siskins and redpolls into even quite small gardens where these trees grow.

Some gardeners dismiss teasels as weeds, but why? They're attractive, easy to grow, and rich in nectar and seeds.

Plants for water and wetland

Flowering rush

Kingcup

Water avens

Water mint

Plants are an indispensable feature of wildlife ponds. They can make a man-made pond seem much more natural, and they provide homes, hiding places, food and breeding facilities for its fascinating, shifting population of residents and visitors. The plant life of a pond also provides a complete recycling service for any waste, as well as keeping the water clean, without the need for costly electrical equipment that has to be installed and regularly maintained. A well-chosen collection of native plants is a key factor in helping a garden pond to operate successfully as a self-contained, balanced ecosystem. Wildlife-friendly pond plants will make your garden look wonderful, too.

Flowering rush
Butomus umbellatus

This native water plant grows best in shallow water at the edge of a medium to large pond. Its beautiful, fragrant pink flowers on tall stems look rather like alliums but flower later in summer. They are followed by purplish seedpods. If flowering rush succeeds in your pond you can divide the rhizome, rather like an iris, to make more plants. Replant the divisions in shallow water, anchoring them in mud or shingle. Take care with the sharp edges of the stems, though.

Kingcup or Marsh marigold
Caltha palustris

A clump of kingcups with their bold, glossy golden flowers open to the sun is among the most uplifting sights of spring. This is one of the few bog plants that makes a strong impact without being too vigorous for a small garden: try planting some in a patch of damp ground beside a wildlife pond. It's easy to please provided it doesn't dry out, and will spread both by seed and by creeping stalks, which root when they touch damp soil. As their wild wetland habitat becomes more and more scarce, kingcups are an especially worthy candidate for nurturing in a wildlife-friendly garden. The flowers provide pollen for bees, and the foliage offers shelter for frogs and other pond creatures.

Water avens
Geum rivale

The charming, nodding flowers of this native marsh plant look lovely beside water, and earn it a place in any dampish corner of the garden. The flowers begin to appear in spring and are followed by attractive feathery seedheads. The garden cultivar 'Leonard's Variety' (shown left) has larger flowers in bright coral, and is a good choice for a cottage-style border.

Water mint
Mentha aquatica

Grow water mint for its scent, above all: it's the most refreshing in the whole garden on a hot summer's day. Like most mints, it is easy to grow, and bees and butterflies enjoy the flowers. Plant it along pond edges where you walk, so that it releases a burst of fragrance when you brush against it as you pass.

Bog bean
Menyanthes trifoliata

This rather special native water plant has leaves shaped like those of a broad bean and spikes of extraordinarily delicate, frilly, pinkish-white flowers that open from attractive pink buds in spring. Plant it at the edge of the pond where it will not dry out; in the wild it grows both in boggy ground and as a dense floating mat on the surface of water.

Water forget-me-not
Myosotis scorpioides

If it establishes happily in your pond, this delightful marginal plant will make a pretty, summery haze of small, yellow-eyed, pale blue forget-me-not flowers above the water. In the wild, it is found in marshy and Fenland regions. Unlike common garden forget-me-nots, it is a perennial plant that spreads by creeping rhizomes as well as by seeding, but it doesn't usually become invasive (though it has become a problem weed in parts of the USA, where it is not native).

Curled pondweed
Potamogeton crispus

Submerged pondweeds, such as this one, play an important role in keeping a pond oxygenated and clean without a pump and filter. Choose with care, though: some non-native pondweeds that are available from aquatic suppliers (such as the Canadian waterweed *Elodea canadensis*) can be too vigorous for an average garden pond. Curled pondweed is a more manageable native, along with spiked water-milfoil (*Myriophyllum spicatum*). Both have underwater stems, with flowers at surface level.

Brooklime
Veronica beccabunga

Once used to combat scurvy, brooklime is an easy, creeping little native plant for pond margins. It is quick to establish, with dark green, healthy-looking leaves that soon provide cover for tadpoles and other small pond creatures. The small speedwell-like flowers – blue with a white eye – attract bees over a long season.

Bog bean

Water forget-me-not

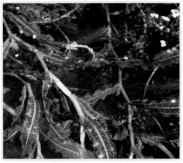
Curled pondweed

Don't buy these!

Conservationists are increasingly worried by the escape of certain non-native water plants from garden ponds into natural watercourses. Many of these are still on sale, but as well as damaging the delicate ecological balance of garden ponds, these aggressive, fast-multiplying plants can be seriously bad news if they invade streams and rivers. This can happen fairly easily, for example in areas that become flooded, or if even the smallest fragment is carelessly disposed of. Small amounts can also be carried from one area of water to another on the feet of birds.

The main species to avoid are:

Water fern or fairy fern (*Azolla filiculoides*)
New Zealand pygmy weed (*Crassula helmsii*)
Water hyacinth (*Eichhornia crassipes*)
Floating pennywort (*Hydrocotyle ranunculoides*)
Curly waterweed (*Lagarosiphon major*)
Water primrose (*Ludwigia grandiflora*, shown right)
Parrot's feather or Brazilian water milfoil (*Myriophyllum aquaticum*)
Water lettuce (*Pistia stratiotes*)

Brooklime

Fungi in the garden

Fungi tend not to get a good press among gardeners. Fungal blights, rusts and moulds may attack plants; fairy rings will disfigure lawns; and the dreaded honey fungus can be fatal to trees and shrubs. But it isn't all bad news. Much of the natural recycling of dead plant material in a garden could not happen without fungi, and some even help plants to grow.

Many of us are fascinated by fungi. They have an extraordinary range of colours and textures, as well as some outlandish names, and they make an intriguing and mysterious addition to the garden scene, especially on those warm, damp autumn days when crops of them have popped up overnight as if by magic. Some, of course, are edible and delicious, but many more are either unpleasant or poisonous – a few

Some garden fungi are easier to identify than others:
① The stuff of fairy tales – the handsome but poisonous fly agaric.
② The aptly named shaggy ink-cap or lawyer's wig, usually seen in grass.
③ Fairy ring toadstools famously grow in circles in lawns and pasture.

to the extent of being deadly. But, that said, a basket of correctly identified fresh parasol or field mushrooms picked from your own grass takes some beating, and if they don't arrive of their own accord you can now buy special kits to cultivate several kinds of home-grown mushrooms.

Extraordinary fungi

Fungi don't have to be edible to be interesting, though, and all kinds of weird and wonderful specimens may be welcome as curiosities when they turn up in gardens.

The enchanting but poisonous red and white fly agaric (*Amanita muscaria*) is always found under birch trees, while the shaggy ink-cap (*Coprinus comatus*), also known as lawyer's wig, sometimes pops up in grass, especially in new lawns. The wood blewit (*Lepista nuda*) is a common species to find among fallen leaves in autumn, while the trunks of mature trees may sprout bracket fungi such as the dryad's saddle (*Polyporus squamosus*) or chicken of the woods (*Laetiporus sulphureus*). Look out, too, for the descriptively named candle-snuff fungus (*Xylaria hypoxylon*), which looks like an extinguished candle wick. It grows in

Don't forget

Never ever eat any fungi unless you are 150% sure of your identification. Poisonous species can cause digestive upsets or even liver damage. So if you aren't sure, don't pick them.

clusters on rotting wood and is sometimes found at the base of old garden fences.

The toadstools that you see in the garden or in the countryside are like the tip of an iceberg. The visible, reproductive part (called the fruiting body) is attached to a much larger organism, whose main part is a collection of fine, thread-like filaments called hyphae that are too small to see with the naked eye. These make up a mass called the mycelium that grows in the soil or inside whatever the fungus is feeding on.

Good and bad fungi

Many fungi in the garden are harmless, feeding on dead plant material such as rotting wood. Some do attack live plants, though. Honey fungus (*Armillaria mellea*) is notorious for its

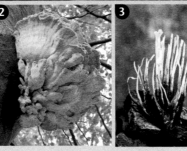

Many woodland fungi attack only rotten wood; others can actually damage or kill plants.

① Honey fungus: just about the most unpopular organism in the garden.

② Chicken of the woods is a bracket fungus that is found on old trees.

③ Look for the little candle-snuff fungus on decaying timber.

Mycorrhizal fungi

Fungi have generally been pretty unwelcome in gardens, but it is now known that certain types in the soil around plant roots can actually help plants because the two have a mutually beneficial relationship. The role of these mycorrhizal fungi in the plant world is beginning to be more widely understood and is turning out to be more important than we ever thought. They function almost like an extra root system for the plant, helping it to absorb the nutrients and water it needs. Plants supported by mycorrhiza tend to establish faster and do better. Many man-made landscapes, however, are lacking in mycorrhiza: intensive cultivation and use of chemical pesticides and fertilizers spoil the structure of the soil and destroy these natural aids to growth. But in the past few years, mycorrhizal fungi have become commercially available to gardeners in the form of a powder, which is sold in packets or tubs. This seems to work well as an environmentally sustainable alternative to fertilizers, helping plants to establish and making it easier for them to extract nutrients and water from the soil.

ability to kill trees and shrubs, and some bracket fungi can cause heart rot in trees. Other, less obvious fungi are responsible for problems such as leaf spots, mildew, the rotting of fruits or roots, 'damping-off' in seedlings, and potato blight. Fungal diseases tend to be more prevalent in wet summers and in humid conditions where air can't circulate freely. Fungi are everywhere. Vast numbers of their tiny spores are carried on the air, waiting for the right conditions to grow on a suitable host, and there's no getting away from them. But in many cases, the best defence against those that can bring disease and death is to grow your

It may seem odd, but plants like clematis are more susceptible to being attacked by mildew if they get dry at the roots.

plants well in the hope that they will be strong enough to resist attack. It's also worth trying disease-resistant varieties: for example, some roses are much less prone to blackspot and some lettuces less susceptible to mildew than others. Peas sown early are less likely to get mildew than ones sown late – in early summer. Mildew can also be deterred by keeping soil moist and by giving plants the light and air they need: don't overcrowd them.

The wildlife in your garden

We've come a long way since the time – not so very long ago – when most gardeners regarded pretty much all the wildlife in their garden as 'the enemy': pests that had to be eliminated in order to keep precious plants in pristine condition. Most of us still find it hard to love a slug or a vine weevil, but there's a welcome trend towards a more relaxed attitude to wildlife, seeing a good garden not as some sort of museum of perfect plants but as an endlessly fascinating community of interdependent living creatures.

Identifying garden wildlife

It's no exaggeration to say that you will never be able to identify all the creatures that you share your garden with. Even a real boffin would be hard-pressed to do a comprehensive naming job on every single one of the many different kinds of moth, beetle and fly that make up the garden's supporting cast. But getting to know the birds, butterflies and pond-dwellers that play the leading parts is a little easier.

The chiffchaff is easily identified by its unmistakable two-note song – an early sign of spring, sometimes heard again in autumn. A similar-looking summer visitor, the willow warbler, has a longer, liquid melody.

Your main assets in becoming familiar with garden wildlife will be sharp observational skills and a clearly illustrated field guide or two (see pages 92–3). A friend or relative with an interest in natural history can also be a big help. The pages that follow should provide a basic introduction to some of your garden residents and visitors, and of course there will be some, or perhaps many, that you already know.

Knowing your regulars

With birds and other larger creatures, the more species you can recognize the easier it becomes to identify others by a process of elimination. The possibilities are comparatively limited, and you'll soon be very familiar with all the regulars, recognizing them as much by their behaviour, their sound, and where and when they appear, as by what they look like – just as you do with people. Birdwatchers call this the 'jizz' of a bird – you just know from experience what it is when you catch the movement or shape out of

the corner of your eye, even when you cannot make out the finer detail such as an eye-stripe. The same can apply to insects. It's hard to mistake a hummingbird hawkmoth, for example, as you watch it hovering and darting in the daytime, feeding from flowers, using its long proboscis to extract the nectar.

Garden wildlife trends

DOING WELL		
Blackbird	Ring-necked parakeet	Honey bee
Blackcap	Sparrowhawk	House martin
Blue tit	Woodpigeon	House sparrow
Collared dove		Mistle thrush
Goldfinch	DECLINING	Redwing
Great spotted woodpecker	Bullfinch	Small tortoiseshell butterfly
Great tit	Common frog	Song thrush
Jackdaw	Dunnock	Spotted flycatcher
Nuthatch	Fieldfare	Stag beetle
Painted lady butterfly	Garden tiger (one of many moths in decline)	Starling
	Hedgehog	Swallow

Frogs depend on water only for breeding. Gardens and their ponds are a real help to these creatures as their populations are increasingly under threat from diseases and habitat loss.

Garden birds

Sparrowhawk

Birds are in the front rank of garden wildlife, and very rewarding they are too. Comparatively large and readily identifiable, they are easy to see and relate to, and they behave in fascinating and entertaining ways. They arrive spontaneously, being able to fly wherever they choose, unimpeded by fences and buildings. They notice, and respond, if we plant trees for them to perch in or put out food and water for them (*see* pages 44–5). We feel honoured if they choose to feed and bathe in our garden, or to raise their families there – and so we should!

Woodpigeon

Sparrowhawk
Accipiter nisus

A sparrowhawk in the garden is an increasingly common sight and provokes mixed feelings: admiration of its extraordinary flying skill and handsome plumage, but distress at the loss of the garden birds on which it preys. Bird feeders are understandably a favourite haunt. Siting feeders close to cover such as a dense hedge, or hanging them inside a large-mesh cage or a structure made of pliable woven twigs, such as willow, may help protect small birds. But a hungry sparrowhawk is a determined creature, especially when it has young to feed, and there is often little you can do.

Collared dove

Woodpigeon
Columba palumbus

Frankly unwelcome in gardens because of its taste for prize cabbages, peas and the tender shoots and blossom of fruit trees in spring, the woodpigeon is nevertheless an intriguing bird. Able to breed pretty well all year round, the bird feeds its young on a special 'milk' that it makes. If woodpigeons do visit your garden, cover your vulnerable crops with netting (*see* pages 50–1) and enjoy the birds for their iridescent plumage and rather comic behaviour: they seem to eat too much to

be agile. Woodpigeons have a white patch on each side of the neck and are bigger than collared doves (left).

Collared dove
Streptopelia decaocto

Whether you find their monotonous calls soothing or irritating, collared doves are a remarkable ornithological success story. As recently as 1955, a carefully guarded breeding pair in East Anglia was a British 'first', and the UK population is now thought to number over half a million. They are supremely opportunist breeders and feeders, sometimes raising young successfully even in winter, and making the most of places where grain and seeds are available, from bird tables and chicken runs to farmyards and arable fields. They also like weed seeds. This dove has a black 'collar' on the back of its neck.

Green woodpecker
Picus viridis

A lawn with a good ant population is the feature most likely to entice one of these splendidly colourful birds into your garden. They have amazingly long, sticky tongues: perfect for extracting ants from their runs. Green woodpeckers are less common than great spotted woodpeckers

Green woodpecker

(right), and are less likely to visit feeders and bird tables. But once you get to know the unmistakable 'laughing' call that gave these birds their familiar name, 'yaffle', you will be much more likely to notice if one of them is about.

Great spotted woodpecker
Dendrocopos major

The great spotted woodpecker, like its green relative, makes a very distinctive sound, especially in spring, by hammering a hollow branch with its bill to produce an extraordinarily loud and resonant drumming. The powerful bill is a key part of the woodpecker's kit, used also to excavate nest holes and to prise beetle larvae out of timber. Great spotted woodpeckers come quite readily to garden nut feeders. Watch closely and you'll see how they cling on with the remarkably strong toes that enable them to gain a foothold on tree trunks. The woodpecker's tail works hard, too, serving as a third 'leg' to help it grip.

Pied wagtail
Motacilla alba

These birds seem to be in a permanent state of bustle, never still for a moment as they rush about on a roof or open area of ground, often near water, with their tails bobbing up and down. This busy lifestyle is partly explained by their diet of tiny

insects: they need to catch an awful lot of them to survive, especially in winter. They live happily in town or country, and sometimes take to garden feeding stations, especially in cold weather, perhaps picking up bits and pieces that have fallen to the ground.

Wren
Troglodytes troglodytes

You'll seldom see a wren at a feeder or bird table, but these rather shy, busy little birds are among the reasons to delay cutting down your perennials until early spring. They like to forage near the ground among twigs, stems and other plant remains, searching out insects and other morsels to keep them alive. Survival in bitter winter weather seems against the odds for such a tiny bird (almost the smallest found in Britain) – just as its song seems impossibly loud. Wrens like to nest in the cover of brushwood or scrub, but may also choose a quiet corner of a shed or outbuilding. The male builds several nests and his partner puts the finishing touches to the one she likes best, lining it with feathers and producing five or six brown-mottled white eggs.

Dunnock
Prunella modularis

Dunnocks used to be known as hedge sparrows: they do like to potter about in hedge bottoms and other shrubby

Great spotted woodpecker

Pied wagtail

Wren

Dunnock

Easy plants to attract birds

Berberis	Flax (*Linum*)
Cotoneaster	Evening primrose (*Oenothera biennis*)
Teasel (*Dipsacus fullonum*)	Wild marjoram (*Origanum vulgare*)
Common ivy (*Hedera helix*)	Poppy (*Papaver*)
Sunflower (*Helianthus annuus*)	Redcurrant (*Ribes rubrum*)

Robin

Blackbird

Song thrush

Blackcap

vegetation, but they're unrelated to sparrows. They are great foragers, and are a good reason for not tidying up too efficiently in the garden. As unobtrusive as mice, they comb through plant debris on the ground in search of seeds and insects. You'll seldom see a dunnock on a bird table, but quite often underneath one, clearing up after the other birds.

Robin
Erithacus rubecula

Needing no introduction, the robin is every gardener's friend. They are plucky and territorial birds, with a distinctive winter song and an eager appreciation of any tasty morsels turned up by a spade or fork, and of a wide range of bird-table foods. The robin's taste in nesting sites is just as varied: hedges, shrubs, holes in trees or in walls, a nook in a shed, or an old kettle or watering can, are all likely nurseries for the broods of up to five spotty, rather grumpy-looking brown babies. These don't have a red breast.

Blackbird
Turdus merula

Garden blackbirds are entertaining to watch as they sort enthusiastically through leaf litter in search of food, or stand with cocked head on a damp lawn before tugging out an earthworm. They are bird-table regulars, eating all kinds of scraps, and enjoying raisins and apples in cold weather. Their enchanting, liquid song is often the first to begin the dawn chorus in spring, and one of the last to fall silent at dusk. Gardens seem to be missing something when blackbirds disappear in late summer to moult, and it's always good to see them back in late autumn, with their smart new plumage.

The crow family

'If you see one rook it's a crow, and if you see more than one crow they're rooks' is a wry old country piece of advice on telling these two common black corvids apart. Also, rooks, unlike crows, have pale skin at the base of the bill. Other crow relatives, such as jays, are much easier to identify. They are a mixed blessing in gardens but hard to deter: magpies and jackdaws (pictured below) are nest robbers, bird-table bullies and seedling thieves (cover those peas and beans!). Jays are more beautiful and fairly shy, but just as opportunistic. All these scavenging family members, however, are valuable pest-control operatives, devouring invertebrates that can damage plants and lawns.

Song thrush
Turdus philomelos

Sadly, this delightful bird is heard less often these days, its decline possibly linked to slug pellets and other garden and farm chemicals. Apart from their uplifting song, characterized by the repetition of each phrase several times, song thrushes attract attention in the garden (especially in dry weather) by the tap-tapping of a snail shell against a stone to get at the juicy mollusc inside. They enjoy winter berries and raisins, but are often driven away by more aggressive blackbirds. The similar but larger mistle thrush has a more densely spotted breast.

Blackcap
Sylvia atricapilla

This sleek, subtly coloured warbler is a wildlife-gardening success story and now regularly overwinters in the UK. Blackcaps tend to be seen singly, or sometimes as a pair, the male true to its name with a jet-black cap, while the female's is chestnut brown. Even a single blackcap is feisty enough to hold its own in the hurly-burly of the bird table, usually choosing soft foods such as apples, suet and cheese. In summer a blackcap is more likely to be heard than seen, singing a varied, melodious song from the leafy cover of a mature tree.

Goldcrest
Regulus regulus

Tiniest of all European birds, the average goldcrest weighs barely 6g (so five goldcrests weigh only an ounce). Their size makes them very vulnerable to prolonged cold weather in winter, though they find a niche in conifers – a habitat that appeals to few other birds. If you have a cypress or yew in your garden, it may well be visited by goldcrests seeking shelter as well as the small insects that they like to eat. Keep an ear open for the very high-pitched calls that betray their presence. If you hear these, stay very still and a goldcrest may well flit into view.

Blue tit
Cyanistes caeruleus

Blue tits are among the most obliging of garden birds: abundant and easy to identify (note the blue head), always entertaining with their acrobatics, and usually appearing right on cue when you hang up a feeder full of peanuts. Hot on pest control, they seek out aphids, small caterpillars and other tiny creatures that lurk among your plants. They are among the easiest birds to coax into breeding in your garden: a suitably located nest box (*see* page 48) with the right size of hole (25mm/1in in diameter) is very likely to be occupied, particularly if your garden has lots of insects to feed the large brood.

Great tit
Parus major

Heralding spring – often while it is still winter for most of us – with its distinctive two-note call ('tea-cher, tea-cher'), the great tit is bigger than the blue tit and has a jet-black head and white cheeks. An easy species to attract to peanut feeders and nest boxes, the great tit is certainly worth encouraging as a breeding bird: a single brood needs several thousand grubs and caterpillars, collected by the long-suffering parents who fly back and forth many times a day while the young are in the nest.

Coal tit
Periparus ater

Coal tits are much less numerous and more shy than blue tits and great tits, but garden birdwatchers will sometimes see them at feeders, or patrolling for insects in summer. A white flash on the back of the head distinguishes these agile little birds from other tits, even from the much rarer marsh tit and willow tit, which are similar in colouring. Coal tits are essentially woodland birds, but they are well adapted to conifers and may be attracted by garden evergreens. They nest in holes and cavities in trees, and may take to a nest box with an opening small enough to exclude bigger birds – 25mm (1in) across, at most.

Goldcrest

Blue tit

Great tit

Coal tit

Long-tailed tit
Aegithalos caudatus

Long-tailed tit

This tiny, acrobatic bird has become increasingly common in gardens and a regular at many peanut feeders, though numbers can be dramatically affected by winter weather. Unmistakable with their pinkish-buff and black plumage and very long tail, they tend to travel about in groups. They are seldom still for a moment as they search for small insects and grubs in the tree canopy, and you often hear the groups before you see them. Long-tailed tits build wonderfully intricate domed nests of moss and feathers. Consider yourself very lucky if you find one: they are always well hidden, often in dense, thorny bushes.

Nuthatch
Sitta europaea

Nuthatch

Get to know the strong, repeated single-note call of a nuthatch high in a tree, and you may find this rather shy woodland bird is more common than you thought. They are most likely to visit gardens near woodland or parkland, with mature trees where nesting holes and food are to be found. The nuthatch uses its sharp, strong bill both to crack nuts and to winkle out insects from underneath tree bark, which is what is likely to be happening if you see one moving down a tree trunk (nearly always down, not up). They also visit nut feeders, sometimes carrying away nuts to hoard.

Treecreeper
Certhia familiaris

Treecreeper

If you are fortunate enough to see a small, mottled brown bird moving up a tree trunk, searching for insects in the crevices in the bark, it is likely to be a treecreeper.

Expert at hiding and camouflage, these birds have fine bills with a distinct downward curve. They are natural woodlanders but will occasionally come to peanut feeders and may roost in the shelter of a garden in severe weather.

Starling
Sturnus vulgaris

Starlings often get a bad press, seen as the greedy bullies of the bird table and sometimes disliked for their large, noisy evening roosts. But they have beautiful mottled, iridescent plumage and an astonishing ability to mimic sounds, from telephones and car alarms to other birds. Starlings like to feed on open ground, such as lawns, and devour soil pests including leatherjackets (cranefly larvae), as well as many kinds of food put out for them. Perhaps surprisingly for such a seemingly successful bird, their numbers are declining everywhere – though British garden populations are swelled in winter by migrant flocks of starlings from northern and eastern Europe.

House sparrow
Passer domesticus

House sparrows used to be seen as a bit of a nuisance in the garden, nibbling tender young plants, making dust-baths in neat seed beds, and elbowing out other small birds. But now that sparrow populations have suffered a mysterious and dramatic decline (by about half), we rather miss the busy chatter and untidy nests that we used to take for granted. The decline has been less marked in suburban areas, where gardens make up a large proportion of the land area, so perhaps gardens are actually helping to conserve these entertaining little birds.

Starling

Chaffinch
Fringilla coelebs

The cheery song of a chaffinch is a familiar soundtrack to that wonderful feeling of optimism on the first warm, sunny days of early spring. Chaffinches have quite broad tastes in food and nesting places, and gardens are good at meeting both these needs. The birds are chiefly seed-eaters, gathering food from trees, grasses and the seedheads of herbaceous plants at different times of the year, and are often spotted pottering along the ground looking for food. Like many seed-eaters, they will also catch and eat insects and spiders in summer when these are plentiful.

Greenfinch
Carduelis chloris

You will often hear greenfinches, with their 'zeee, zeee, zeee' call. Attracted to peanuts and sunflower seeds in bird feeders, they also like to forage on the ground and are fond of many garden seeds and fruits. They nest in conifers

and other evergreen shrubs and trees. Greenfinches have been affected recently by a parasitic disease that can be spread in drinking water and at feeding stations. There is no cure but good bird-feeder hygiene can help prevent it. The siskin is similar to the greenfinch but is smaller, with more obviously streaked plumage.

Goldfinch
Carduelis carduelis

It's always exciting to see these exotic-looking little finches, with their red faces and bright yellow wing-bars. They are enthusiastic seed-feeders and move about readily in search of suitable food, so it can be quite easy to attract them into the garden. Teasels seldom fail, and they enjoy the seeds of many other plants including thistles, daisies and dandelions, groundsel and *Eryngium*. Commercially produced Niger seed is also worth trying. Goldfinches often nest high in trees, sometimes surprisingly late in summer, eventually emerging to feed in a busy, softly chattering family group.

House sparrow

Chaffinch

Greenfinch

Goldfinch

Whose egg?

TYPE OF BIRD	SIZE OF EGG	EGG COLOUR	NUMBER OF EGGS
Blackbird	Medium-sized	light greenish blue with brown streaks	up to 4 in a clutch
Blue tit	Tiny	white speckled with reddish brown	up to 15
Chaffinch	Smallish	variously coloured and streaked	up to 6
Collared dove	Medium-sized	white	usually 2
Great tit	Small	white speckled with reddish brown	up to 10
House sparrow	Smallish	whitish with dark blotches	up to 5
Robin	Smallish	whitish buff with gingery blotches and speckles	up to 5
Starling	Medium-sized	light blue	up to 7
Woodpigeon	Large	white	usually 2
Wren	Tiny	white, lightly speckled brown	up to 6

Pond life

Pond watching on a sunny day can be an utterly absorbing and stress-relieving activity. You'll need a good field guide to identify all the creatures you see, and perhaps a hand lens if you plan to do some pond dipping. These pages will start you off, giving just a taster of the rich variety of life that may be found in and around even a small garden pond.

Emperor dragonfly

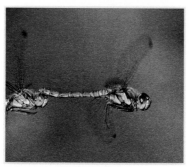

Common darter

Damselfly

Freshwater snail

Dragonflies

A delicate, jewel-like dragonfly in the sunshine is one of the most thrilling sights for pond owners. Dragonflies are adept at finding water and you may even be lucky enough to attract the largest British species, the fast-flying emperor dragonfly. The male is bright blue with a black line, and holds its body slightly bowed in flight. A smaller blue and green dragonfly you may see is the southern hawker, while the common darter is smaller again, and orange-brown: one of several similar species. About the same size, with blue males and brown females, is the broad-bodied chaser – one of the likeliest to breed in a garden pond. Dragonfly eggs are laid in underwater plant stems, in silt, or in the water, according to species. The eggs develop into nymphs that really are among the 'ugly ducklings' of the garden. It may take years of voracious feeding on other pond creatures, and regularly shedding its skin to accommodate its increasing bulk, before a nymph finally crawls up a plant stem. Then, a slow and truly extraordinary transformation takes place as it dries, sheds its drab adolescent garb and unfolds to emerge into its short but beautiful existence as an adult.

Damselflies

Damselflies are distinguished from true dragonflies by their dainty, more slender bodies and by the position of their wings when resting: a dragonfly holds its wings at right angles to its body, while a damselfly folds its wings along its back. Some damselflies prefer moving water, but those most likely to be seen around garden ponds include several similar blue species, such as the blue-tailed damselfly, the common blue damselfly and the azure damselfly. The large red damselfly is also quite common and widespread around still water.

Freshwater snails

Snails make an important contribution to a pond's ecosystem, helping to keep the water clean by grazing on algae and scavenging on other detritus. One of the largest is the great pond snail, conspicuous on its regular trips up to the surface of the water for air. Other common snails include the wandering snail and the spiral-shelled ramshorn and great ramshorn.

Great diving beetle
Dytiscus marginalis

Great diving beetles fly around after dark and soon discover new ponds. Both adults and their larvae are among the more impressive pond-dwellers, and both are voracious carnivores, attacking tadpoles, small fish and even newts with relish. They swim strongly, helped by the paddle-like hairs on their back legs, and

Aquatic larvae

As well as dragonflies and damselflies (*see* opposite), many smaller flies also breed in ponds. They include mosquitoes, whose larvae, like tiny thin tadpoles, soon appear in any still water in summer. Caddis flies package their underwater larvae in special tubular cases, disguised with materials from seeds and fragments of wood to sand grains or pieces of snail shell. The aptly named rat-tailed maggot, whose 'tail' is a breathing tube that enables it to tolerate stagnant water, is the aquatic larva of the drone fly, a common and much less sinister bee-lookalike. Other insects prefer running water, such as stoneflies and most kinds of mayfly.

are easily seen on their frequent visits to the water surface to take in air through their tails. They are completely aquatic and if a pond dries up they will either move away or burrow into the mud.

Whirligig beetle
Gyrinus natator

These engaging little pond creatures are unmistakable and well named, twirling energetically about in gangs on the water's surface. The structure of their eyes is unusual – they have 'bifocal' vision, which enables them to see both above and below the water. Be thankful if whirligig beetles arrive in your pond because, quite apart from their entertainment value, their favourite meal is mosquito larvae.

Pond skater
Gerris lacustris

Fascinating to watch for their ability to walk on water, pond skaters achieve this remarkable feat by trapping air among the hairy pads on the underside of their legs. This enables them to avoid breaking the surface tension of the water. Pond skaters live on small insects unlucky enough to land on the water's surface, which they detect from a distance and then catch with their strong front legs. The longer middle pair serves as oars, and the rear pair acts as a rudder.

Water boatman or Backswimmer
Notonecta glauca

Resembling a tiny single-scull oarsman, this common water bug is unlike many aquatic creatures in being able to fly rather well. Although it is just as happy under the water, it has to breathe air, which it does by trapping bubbles in the hairs beneath its wings and on its legs, on regular visits to the water's surface. It is sometimes seen literally 'hanging about', just below the water's surface, but the slightest disturbance from a potential nearby meal such as an insect, tiny fish or tadpole can immediately send it into hunting mode. And be warned: this water bug has a painful bite, too.

Great diving beetle

Whirligig beetles

Pond skater

Water boatman

Pond dipping

You're sure to see interesting aquatic life from the edges of your pond, but a few minutes spent with a sieve, a shallow white tray and a hand lens will reveal much more. First, pour a little clear pond water into the tray. Swish the sieve (or net) very gently in the pond, trying to avoid too much weed and mud. Tip the contents into the tray to look with the lens at any creatures you may have caught. Put the results of each 'dip' back into the pond, and repeat the process in another part of the pond to see if you get different results.

Amphibians and reptiles

It's odd that such a bunch of harmless and fascinating creatures as our native amphibians and reptiles should be so unappealing to some people. Why not overcome your prejudices and make friends with them? As wild habitats disappear, garden ponds (*see* pages 36–9) can ensure the survival of these wonderful creatures, which are strong allies in the battle against slugs and other living things on the gardener's 'unloved' list.

Common frog

Common toad

Whose spawn?

Frog spawn is laid in blobs near the water's surface in early spring. Toad spawn, which is deposited later and deeper, is laid in long strings.

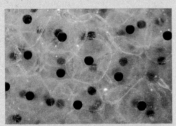

Frog spawn

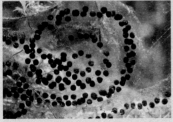

Toad spawn

Common frog
Rana temporaria

Encourage frogs into your garden with an accessible, amphibian-friendly pond. Size hardly matters, nor does depth (a few centimetres will do), but gently sloping sides are essential to allow the frogs to get in and out. Once you have frogs they will, with luck, return to spawn in their birthplace on the first mild days of each year. They will then reward you with a few days of their best singing ('croaking' is a harsh term for such a gentle sound), and with lots of lovely spawn, followed by tadpoles and eventually tiny frogs. Frogs usually lay their spawn in abundant quantities, but only a tiny percentage of the little black dots will eventually become adult frogs; spawn, tadpoles and froglets alike are popular meals for certain birds, grass snakes, and carnivorous pond creatures, including newts. Make sure that there is plenty of vegetation around the pond for surviving froglets to hide in after they emerge in late spring. Frogs, unlike toads, have smooth skin and their hind legs are longer. These enable them to jump (and, sometimes, even make you jump!) extremely effectively.

Common toad
Bufo bufo

Toads are sometimes described in less than complimentary terms, but they are useful creatures that eat slugs and snails. Their skin may be 'warty' but they have beautiful, jewel-like golden eyes that few people notice. After toads come out of hibernation in spring, they migrate in remarkably large numbers to their breeding ponds, sometimes travelling long distances and encountering many dangers, such as busy roads, on the way. They visit water only to spawn, usually arriving a little later than frogs, and laying their spawn deeper in the water, so toad spawn is less conspicuous. The toads disperse after spawning to lead solitary lives, and at other times of year you are likely to find them under stones, or perhaps in your greenhouse or vegetable garden – which is to be encouraged. They are most active at night, emerging to catch their prey with long, sticky tongues.

Threatened amphibians

Frog numbers in Britain and elsewhere have fallen worryingly over recent years. Loss of ponds in the countryside is a key reason for the decline, but many species of amphibians worldwide are being wiped out by two incurable diseases. For this reason, conservationists now recommend that amphibians should be left to colonize new garden ponds spontaneously: if you bring in spawn or tadpoles from elsewhere, you may be unwittingly introducing viral or fungal infections. The website of the conservation charity Froglife (www.froglife.org) has more information on the diseases and suggests what you should do if you find sick or dead frogs or toads.

Smooth newt
Triturus vulgaris

Also known as the common newt, this is the one you are most likely to have in your pond in spring: look out for the wavy crest from neck to tail and the dashing orange tummy of the male at breeding time. When in the water, newts behave rather like minute crocodiles, hunting for tadpoles and other water creatures. Outside the breeding season newts can be found almost anywhere, from woods to gardens to damp sheds or cellars. They hibernate underground during the coldest months.

Slow-worm
Anguis fragilis

Beautiful, harmless and a true gardener's friend, think of slow-worms as legless lizards (which they are), not snakes nor indeed worms. But, unfortunately for them, they really are slow: too slow, sometimes, to avoid garden machinery. So, to keep them safe, go easy with that strimmer, especially in quiet corners with longer grass. And if you're lucky enough to have slow-worms, encourage them to stay by providing a suitable home: a pile of small logs, an undisturbed compost heap, and perhaps a sheet of corrugated iron in a sunny place, where they can shelter, warm up, and be safe from predators such as cats. They will reward you by devouring your slugs. Unless you are skilled, don't try to pick up a slow worm: true to its Latin species name *fragilis*, it may well shed its tail as a defensive reaction. The tail eventually regrows in part, but the stumpy new version will never look quite the same. Slow-worms can live for many years – if they manage to dodge the numerous hazards that beset them.

Grass snake
Natrix natrix

A grass snake in your pond or compost heap is something to be really proud of. They are strikingly handsome animals – greenish with a smart yellow collar. Although they can look rather fearsome, sometimes growing to well over a metre in length, grass snakes are completely harmless. (Britain's only venomous snake, the adder, is an unlikely garden visitor.) They shed their skins several times a year, and a sloughed skin may be the first sign of a grass snake's presence in the garden. They like warm places in which to lay their eggs and will travel a long distance in search of just the right spot: a compost heap that warms up successfully may prove an ideal location.

Common lizard
Lacerta vivipara

The common lizard is widespread in Britain, and probably lives in many more gardens than we think – it is very shy and well camouflaged, so is easily overlooked. Look out for lizards on sunny days, when they love to sunbathe on a warm bank or wall; but be quiet and don't make any sudden movements, as they will scuttle away at the slightest cause for alarm. Lizards are 10–16cm (4–6in) long and prey enthusiastically on various creepy-crawlies such as beetles, flies and caterpillars. They give birth to anything up to ten young, each arriving neatly parcelled in a transparent sac that breaks at birth. The young lizards are like miniature versions of their parents, but much darker and with shorter tails. Like other reptiles, lizards shed the surface layer of skin periodically as they increase in size, and they can also shed their tails in order to escape danger.

Smooth newt

Slow-worm

Grass snake

Common lizard

The pleasure of watching wildlife will be greatly enhanced if you arrange things so that you can observe your garden visitors at close quarters, in comfort and, most important, without disturbing them. Ways of achieving this range from a thoughtfully planned garden layout, through equipping yourself with a few basic pieces of kit, to the simple but vital tactic of keeping still and quiet.

Observing birds and pond life

A pond and a feeding station that are visible from the windows you most often look out of will give you a sense of involvement with your garden wildlife throughout the year. Regular wildlife watching from the house means you're less likely to miss those special but fleeting events such as the appearance of a newly hatched dragonfly or the sight of recently arrived swallows at the edge of your pond gathering mud for their nests.

It's always very rewarding to be able to watch birds at close range – especially from indoors on a cold day. Transparent window feeders can either be fixed to the sill or stuck to the glass

A pondside gazebo makes a cool and pleasant summer retreat in the garden, and enables you to watch wildlife without being noticed.

with suction cups. Alternatively, hang an ordinary nut or seed holder close to the window. It may take a while for birds to come close, but they will get used to you in time, so persevere, and try not to frighten them away by sudden movements or noises. Blackbirds, robins, chaffinches, greenfinches, great tits and blue tits are all relatively tame and will visit window feeders, and you may get close-up views of some more unusual species. And in springtime, a nest box camera fitted to a nest box or feeding station can be linked either wirelessly or with suitable wiring to your computer or TV for close-up views of the action in your bird garden.

In the garden itself, position a seat for summer wildlife watching. A shady arbour with a view of a sunny pond or bird table is ideal, making you less

Fit a camera to a blue tit nesting box, and you'll be completely enthralled by close-up views of the unfolding drama from egg-laying to fledging.

conspicuous and ensuring that your visitors are in full light for easier observation and identification. Keen wildlife watchers with space in the garden may even decide to build themselves a simple hide. This could be a modest, temporary structure of fabric or woven willow, or a small shed, summerhouse or gazebo, but make sure it's sturdy enough to stand up to wind and rain.

Using binoculars

A pair of binoculars will make all the difference to your wildlife watching. Lightweight types are the most practical, and ones with larger objective lenses (40mm or 50mm) gather more light and will give a much better view on dull days. High magnification (greater than 10) tends to mean more weight and less light, so choose a pair with a magnification no greater than 7 or 8: 7x40 or 8x50 may be the best specifications to try first.

Examining insects and other mini-beasts

A hand lens is a useful piece of kit for examining and identifying small creatures – or at least, the ones that don't run or fly away at your approach. For example, it's worth looking closely at tree trunks to spot any moths that are taking a daytime rest there, and to marvel at their amazing camouflage skills. A simple, inexpensive 'bug box' (a transparent plastic pot with a magnifying lid) makes it easy to get a close look at other, less passive insects before releasing them. These pots make good presents for children, as does a 'pooter' – a clear jar with two

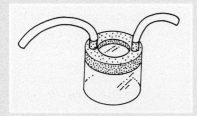

A pooter provides an easy way to catch small insects to look at.

Wildlife gardens never sleep, and there's nearly always something to see after dark.

① Hedgehogs are surprisingly tolerant of being watched as night falls, but do move slowly and quietly to avoid startling them.

② On landing, the large yellow underwing moth quickly tucks its hindwings away beneath the drab upperwings, making it very hard to spot.

flexible tubes projecting through the lid. You place the far end of one above a small spider, beetle or bug, for example, and suck gently on the other, and the creature is sucked into the jar where you can inspect it in more detail before letting it go as soon as you can, preferably in a place where it will not be vulnerable to predators.

The night watch

A dim garden light that you can occasionally switch on at dusk may enable you to watch hedgehogs and other creatures of the night (with the inside lights off, of course). Choose a mild, damp evening in late spring or summer to go out in the hope of seeing bats at their amazing aerobatics. They move too fast to be seen in detail, and it's hard to identify them by species without a special electronic bat detector that picks up the different frequencies of the various kinds. Moths are most likely to be attracted to house or garden lights on warm, still evenings. Again, they may not keep still long enough for you to see them clearly, but you will often find some tucked away indoors or in the garden the following morning and you may be able to identify them with the help of a book or the internet.

Identifying and recording species

For identification there's no substitute for a good field guide. Various general guides are available that cover garden birds, insects, animals and so on in a single volume. Identifying birds both by plumage and by their song is covered by various DVDs, too. Garden insects are so numerous that you will find a more specialized book really helpful. Make sure it shows the larval stages (for example the great variety of butterfly and moth caterpillars) as well as the adults.

Recording your finds in digital photographs, sketches and notes will help you to remember species and steadily increase your knowledge of the natural world. And if you keep a diary with a page to record sightings and developments for each day or week of the year, you can add to it year by year and then look back to compare one season with another.

Small mammals

Bank vole

Most mammals are a mixed blessing in gardens. They eat things we'd rather they didn't: mice are partial to beans and bulbs, squirrels steal peanuts, and scavenging urban foxes may unpack your rubbish in search of leftovers. Even keen wildlife gardeners vary in their appreciation of these creatures, and when it boils down to it, whether we give priority to voles or crocuses is a personal choice. It's certainly true, however, that the more you get to know these animals and understand their behaviour, the more fascinating they become.

Wood mouse

Yellow-necked mouse

Common shrew

Voles

The bank vole and the field (or short-tailed) vole are fairly common but you'd probably need to see them side by side to tell them apart. Bank voles (*Clethrionomys glareolus*) have redder fur, longer tails and bigger ears. They are the more likely of the two to be found in gardens, building their nests – usually made of grass – underground or in a compost heap. Voles are fond of seeds, nuts and berries, but also seedlings and the green stems of young trees and climbing beans. They'll nibble root crops too. Many garden crimes blamed on mice are actually the work of voles.

Wood mouse
Apodemus sylvaticus

Wood mice (also known as long-tailed field mice) do inhabit woods and yet are now more common in our gardens, sheds and homes than house mice. They are probably Britain's most numerous small mammals. The large black eyes, alert ears (useful on nocturnal forays) and twitching whiskers all conspire to create a creature that looks impossibly cute, but sadly no mouse is a reliable friend to the gardener. During cold weather, especially, mice find seeds, nuts, fruit and young shoots just too hard to resist!

Yellow-necked mouse
Apodemus flavicollis

The yellow-necked mouse's name really does help to identify it: the adult has a yellowish-orange band across the paler fur under its chin. This is Britain's largest and most impressive mouse. Indeed, a large adult can be as big as a small rat. Yellow-necked mice are found in houses and sheds, especially in winter, and when we think we have rats, we may instead have a family of noisy, yellow-necked mice. Like all mice, they eat seeds and bulbs, and spoil stored fruit or potatoes.

Common shrew
Sorex araneus

Shrews are common but difficult to observe because they spend much of their time underground and are always moving at great speed. They have to forage all the time since their metabolism is so fast that they die without constant feeding. They are short-lived and largely carnivorous, eating mainly soil-dwelling creatures such as earthworms and chafer grubs. You can tell a shrew by its long, pointed nose, and you are most likely to see one quite by chance, or you might just hear its squeaks as it tears about. The squeaks become louder when two shrews meet – they don't like company.

Bats

If you have bats hunting over your garden from late spring onwards, count yourself very lucky. These harmless mammals have suffered a frightening fall in numbers, probably due to loss of both habitat and breeding places. Bats are choosy about roosting and breeding sites (see page 48), and one of the best things you can do for them is to encourage plenty of night-flying insects. A pond (see pages 36–9) and nectar-rich plants (see pages 70–1) are a good start. You are unlikely to be able to tell which species you have as they flit overhead but in many parts of the country the tiny common pipistrelle (Pipistrellus pipistrellus) is the most common. It weighs less than a £1 coin, but can still eat several thousand insects in one night. All 17 bat species in the UK are protected by law. The Bat Conservation Trust is the organization to approach for expert advice, for example about building work that may affect an existing bat roost. If a bat flies into your house, don't try to catch it. The best thing to do is to switch off the lights and open the windows. It will usually find its way out quite quickly.

Grey squirrel
Sciurus carolinensis

Like them or loathe them (many bird lovers are in the latter camp), grey squirrels are a fixture in countless rural, suburban and town gardens. Feelings run high: they are clearly loved by many wildlife watchers in parks and gardens, and their crimes as egg thieves and tree-chewers may be overlooked. You might smile at their antics as they steal nuts from your bird feeder, but will you feel the same if you catch one taking eggs or even young from a robin's nest? (See also page 51.)

Hedgehog
Erinaceus europaeus

Gardens that aren't too tidy are ideal for hedgehogs, offering cover for nesting and hibernation, dead leaves for snug bedding, a supply of slugs, worms and beetles to eat, and sometimes even a sympathetic human to leave out cat food or scraps as a treat (but never milk, which can upset their digestion). Hedgehogs aren't usually seen by day but their presence is given away after dusk by grunting, snuffling and munching sounds as they potter about. They are a delight to watch, not usually minding the light of a dim torch, and if you keep very still they may well be undeterred by your presence. If you see a hibernating hedgehog while gardening in winter, try not to disturb it, and never light a bonfire, or move compost or leaf mould, without checking the heap first. Hedges offer these creatures shelter for nesting or hibernation, and safe access from one garden to another. (See also page 47.)

Rabbit
Oryctolagus cuniculus

Sitting on someone else's grass, rabbits look charming. But most gardeners really do not want these mega-efficient chewers (and breeders) on their patch. They can inflict real damage on shrubs and trees, not to mention vegetables and flowers. Thankfully, they do seem to like some plants less than others, so grow aromatic herbs, euphorbias with irritant sap, and toxic plants like monkshoods, foxgloves and arums. Rabbits also tend to dislike peonies, sedums, catmint and penstemons, and some bulbs such as snowdrops and narcissi. However, the best course of action is to keep rabbits on the other side of a fence. (See also pages 50–1.)

Common pipistrelle

Grey squirrel

Hedgehog

Rabbit

Insects and other mini-beasts

Honey bee

Bumblebee

Wasps

Hoverfly

Everyone expects and welcomes visiting butterflies and bees, but it might surprise you to learn that a single garden could contain several thousand different kinds of insects and other small creeping or flying creatures. You'll never see, let alone identify, the great majority of your garden's smaller inhabitants, but once you get to know the more obvious ones, you soon realize that there's a whole endlessly intriguing world out there.

Bees

Honey bees and bumblebees are social, as opposed to the many garden species that are solitary, such as leaf-cutter bees. Most honey bees are kept in hives but a swarm from a wild colony can take up residence in a hollow tree or other suitable space. Honey bees are famed for the fascinating, sophisticated organization of their colonies. After she has mated with the male drones, who have no other role, the queen's job is to lay all the eggs. Worker bees (sterile females) collect nectar and pollen to feed the queen, the drones and larvae. They also make wax to build and seal new cells and take care of housework, as well as defending the colony.

Like honey bees, bumblebees live in colonies, but generally nest in the ground. They favour sunny, undisturbed hedge bottoms, compost heaps, long grass and banks. They operate in a similar way to honey bees, but all except the young queens die at the end of each season. New queens emerge from hibernation in early spring, visiting flowers to top up with nectar before choosing a nest site. The large bumblebees that fly on fine days in early spring are most likely to be queens of the buff-tailed bumblebee – one of only 6 out of 25 British species that are still common after some 50 years of declining bee populations.

Superficially similar to bumblebees are the several kinds of cuckoo bee, so called because they take over bumblebees' nests and lay their own eggs in them, often killing the queen bumblebee. The parasites then make use of their unfortunate host's worker bees and food store to rear their own young. Cuckoo bees therefore need no workers of their own, nor do they have the 'pollen baskets' that bumblebees use to collect pollen on their legs, as their pollen is collected for them. Each species of cuckoo bee looks like the bumblebee species that it parasitizes, but the bodies of cuckoo bees are less densely hairy and more shiny than those of bumblebees – they don't need the hairs to pick up pollen.

Wasps

Being stung by a wasp can be very unpleasant, but most are not aggressive and will sting only if they feel threatened

Helping bees

The recent catastrophic decline in honey-bee populations, with the sudden deaths of many whole colonies, is still something of a mystery. This is a serious problem not just for the bees but also for us – commercial food crops and other plants depend on bees for pollination. Gardeners can offer valuable help to all bees by stopping the use of insecticides, and by providing nectar-rich plants (see pages 70–1 and 102) that flower over a long season so that there is always something for visiting bees to feed on.

or if you surprise or provoke them. Their visits may still be most unwelcome on your picnic, but they actually do a lot of good in gardens, feeding their young on caterpillars and other soft insects that might otherwise be eating your plants. As with bees, there are solitary and social wasps, and many different species of both of these. You may see wasps scraping the surface of wood: they use it to make a papery substance for building their intricate cellular nests.

Hoverflies

There are numerous different species of hoverfly and even experts find it hard to tell them apart. Many resemble bees and wasps, so predators are wary of them – a clever ruse. The larvae of many of the common species feed on aphids, so they're hugely valuable in the garden. Adult hoverflies feed on nectar and pollen, and this is the secret of attracting them to your garden. They need their nectar to be easily accessible, so flat, open flowers are the best (*see* pages 102–3).

Lacewings

Look after your lacewings: these delicate-looking insects, sometimes found in a shed or garage where they have tucked themselves up for the winter, are real garden allies. A single lacewing can eat hundreds of aphids during its lifetime: despite their fragile appearance, both adults and larvae are greedy predators. The larvae of green lacewings hatch from eggs that you may be able to spot on stalks, leaves and plant stems: the female attaches each egg with a thin, sticky thread that she produces. Lacewings mostly fly at night, when they may be attracted to house or garden lights. (*See also* page 103.)

Bush-crickets

Long, fine antennae distinguish bush-crickets from grasshoppers, which prefer open grassy meadows to gardens. But the brownish, dark bush-cricket will sunbathe happily on garden shrubs or brambles. The handsome green oak bush-cricket likes tree cover during the day, but may be attracted to house and street lights at night. Many (but not all) male bush-crickets sing audibly in summer; others attract a mate by tapping a foot on a leaf or twig. They are harmless in gardens.

Shield bugs

Shield bugs are among the more conspicuous garden bugs, and are named for the general shape of their bodies. Illustrated together in an insect book, they look like an array of little multi-coloured heraldic shields, patterned in shades of bronze, green and reddish brown. The largest, the hawthorn shield bug, is about 1cm (½ in) long, and the bugs like to bask on leaves on warm days. They are relatively harmless in gardens.

Woodlice

Found in almost every garden, woodlice are, surprisingly, part of the crustacean family. They lurk in damp places, under stones and timber, and will suffocate if their skins get too dry. Another unusual feature of woodlice is that they give birth to live young, carrying their eggs around in a pouch. Woodlice have an 'external' skeleton, like a prawn's shell, which is cast off as they grow and can sometimes be found among garden debris. Woodlice are effective waste-disposal systems for dead plant material and just occasionally attack young seedlings, usually in greenhouses and frames.

Lacewing

Oak bush-cricket

Green shield bug

Woodlouse

Cockchafer

Violet ground beetle

Common garden spider

Crab spider

Beetles

Beetles form a huge sub-group of insects and there are several thousand species in the British Isles alone. They vary enormously in shape, size and colour, but most have hard protective wing-cases and prefer to walk rather than fly. Some beetles, such as ladybirds, are carnivorous while others, such as weevils, chafers and leaf beetles, are plant-eaters. The larvae of longhorn beetles and bark beetles are among those that feed on wood.

Many beetles are nocturnal, but some are more conspicuous by day, especially those that like to sun themselves. Typical of these are the red cardinal beetles and red-and-black soldier or sailor beetles. On a warm, sunny day, the flowerheads of umbelliferous plants, such as parsley and hogweed, are a good place to spot them lying in wait for smaller insects that are attracted to the flowers.

In contrast to these sun-loving beetles are the ground beetles, which burrow in the earth or under stones during the day and emerge after dark. The violet ground beetle is quite common in gardens and a useful night-time predator of slugs. The rove beetles include the rather forbidding-looking devil's coach horse, which spends its days in dark, damp places under stones and in compost heaps. It, too, comes out at night to patrol garden paths and beds for slugs and smaller insects.

Spiders

Most small garden life forms are far more complex and interesting than they may at first appear, and spiders are no exception. Several hundred species of spider live in Britain. They are divided into a number of groups or families with some very different characteristics and behaviour. All of them feed mainly on live insects such as flies, which they catch in a variety of intriguing ways. Many of the spiders that are found outdoors do not use webs to catch their prey.

Some, such as the aptly named zebra spider, are fast-moving hunters, and are often seen stalking insects on sunny walls before pouncing on one – hence the term

Ladybirds: spot the difference

Seven-spot ladybird

Harlequin ladybird

The familiar ladybird has long been a staunch garden friend: most types and their larvae are very partial to aphids. Unfortunately, an alien ladybird that can easily out-compete and even attack the various native species has spread rapidly throughout the country. These harlequin ladybirds are larger and rounder than most native ladybirds, but identifying them is tricky because both native and harlequin ladybirds vary greatly in colour and pattern. However, the familiar native seven-spot ladybird (*Coccinella 7-punctata*) is the only one with exactly seven spots on a red background, so you can safely welcome this one into your garden.

'jumping spiders' to describe this group, which can be fascinating to watch. In another group of hunting spiders are the wolf spiders, so named as they were thought to hunt in packs. Another larger hunting spider, the nursery web spider, makes a web not to catch prey but as a sort of silken tent to rear its young in.

The common garden spider belongs to a group known as orb web spiders. Larger and more round than the zebra spider, it is often seen, with its web, on shrubs and other garden vegetation in summer and autumn. Its body is attractively and variably marked. Crab spiders are also often found in gardens, usually among flowers or leaves. Some species have a fascinating ability to camouflage themselves by changing to white, green or yellow, to blend in with the flower in which they lie in wait for their prey.

Often mistaken for spiders but in fact quite different are the delicate, long-legged creatures known as harvestmen. They are just as much the gardener's friends as the spiders, preying on a range of insects and mites, and even small slugs and snails. Unlike spiders, harvestmen dislike dry heat, preferring the cool, damp shade of leaf litter or other vegetation.

Mites

Mites are a large group of spider relatives. Many are too tiny to see, but countless numbers of them live in garden soil. Some feed on plant material, others are parasites or carnivores, eating creatures even smaller than themselves. Velvet mites are the most likely to be seen in the garden. They are large and bright red, and scurry about very visibly on warm walls and paths. The much smaller red spider mites can be serious plant pests, especially in greenhouses.

Slugs

Surely there is nothing good to say about slugs, whether you are a gardener or not? Making a case for slugs is tough but many do an important job in the garden by eating dead and decaying vegetable matter, and some of our favourite creatures, such as hedgehogs, find slugs tasty. Slugs range from the impressive large, patterned leopard slug (also known as the great grey slug), which eats mainly fungus, to the smaller but much more damaging netted slug and garden slug. All are most active on mild nights after rain – a good time to go out with a torch and remove them from choice plants. To restrict their numbers, put down beer or citrus-peel traps and encourage slug predators (*see* page 53).

Snails

Snails are just as unwelcome as slugs in most gardens: one of the most common species, the garden snail, can very quickly ruin young plants, although many snails prefer dead and decaying vegetable matter. Tiny marvels of design, snails get about using their slimy, built-in conveyor belt, and their retractable stalked eyes are very sensitive to light, sound and touch. Like slugs, they attract some of our favourite garden creatures, such as the song thrush (*see* page 84), which seeks out snails especially in dry weather. You will sometimes hear a thrush hammering a snail shell on a stone to break it and extract the soft flesh. Many snails are true hermaphrodites, but they must mate to produce their small pearly eggs, which are sometimes to be found in dark, damp corners. Unlike most slugs, snails are sometimes found quite high up in trees, where they may shelter in cracks and crevices when it's dry or cold.

Velvet mite

Leopard slug

Garden slug eggs

Garden snail

Brimstone

Holly blue

Peacock

Painted lady

Butterflies

Comparatively few kinds of butterfly breed on garden plants, but gardens with a varied mixture of flowers are likely to attract a range of nectar-seeking adults at different times of the year. It's always a joy to see a brimstone butterfly dancing in the spring sunshine, often near primroses and other early nectar-bearing plants. Brimstones are much harder to spot when at rest, as their folded wings can look just like a yellowish-green leaf. The food plant of their green caterpillars is buckthorn (*Rhamnus* – reflected in the butterfly's name *Gonepteryx rhamni*) and alder buckthorn: even one or two buckthorn plants may attract egg-laying females in late spring.

Along with peacocks, commas and small tortoiseshells, brimstones are among the few butterflies that spend winter as adults. Waiting under dense evergreen vegetation, or in dark corners of sheds and houses, they emerge at the first sign of warmth. If you find a hibernating butterfly in winter, try to keep it cool and dark to help it survive until the spring.

Other resident butterfly species overwinter as an egg or a caterpillar, or a well-hidden chrysalis. The last group include another early garden visitor, the orange-tip. You'll see it from mid-spring onwards, usually not far from its food plants such as honesty or the cuckoo flower – look closely for its single orange eggs. The holly blue butterfly also overwinters as a chrysalis, unlike its relatives the common blue, chalkhill blue and brown argus. These are mainly grassland butterflies, but the holly blue finds what it needs in gardens: holly for its first brood, in spring, and ivy for its second, in late summer.

Most of the group commonly known as the 'browns', which includes the ringlet,

Butterfly food plants

Small tortoiseshell caterpillars in nettles

Adult butterflies feed on a wide range of nectar-rich garden flowers (*see* pages 70–1), but their caterpillars are much fussier. The relationships between caterpillars and their favourite plants are complex, depending on factors such as the location as well as the species of the plant. But it's safe to say that certain food plants do tend to be favoured by the caterpillars of certain butterflies. Gardeners know only too well that the large and small white butterflies always head for your cabbage patch, but here are a few less controversial butterflies and some of their favoured food plants:

BRIMSTONE: buckthorn (*Rhamnus cathartica*); alder buckthorn (*Frangula alnus*)

COMMA: hop (*Humulus lupulus*); stinging-nettle (*Urtica dioica*); currants and gooseberry

GATEKEEPER, MEADOW BROWN, RINGLET, SPECKLED WOOD: grasses

HOLLY BLUE (spring): holly (*Ilex aquifolium*)

HOLLY BLUE (summer): ivy (*Hedera helix*)

ORANGE-TIP: cuckoo flower (*Cardamine pratensis*); sweet rocket (*Hesperis matronalis*); honesty (*Lunaria annua*)

PAINTED LADY: thistles (various species of *Cirsium* and *Carduus*)

PEACOCK: stinging-nettle (*Urtica dioica*)

RED ADMIRAL: stinging-nettle (*Urtica dioica*)

SILVER-WASHED FRITILLARY: dog violet (*Viola riviniana*)

SMALL TORTOISESHELL: stinging-nettle (*Urtica dioica*)

gatekeeper and meadow brown, and also (confusingly) the marbled white, feed on grasses. These butterflies hibernate as small caterpillars, emerging to munch grass stems on late-spring evenings and pupating around midsummer.

Among our most familiar garden butterflies are two that do not normally overwinter in Britain. Both the red admiral and the painted lady fly here in spring from the warmer climate of North Africa or the Mediterranean. Some years see a huge influx of painted ladies, especially near the coast of southern England, when incredible numbers swarm in after their arduous sea crossing. These migrant butterflies breed here, and their offspring form a new crop of adults, which stock up on nectar from buddleia bushes and sunny flower beds in late summer before the long flight south.

Moths

There are certain to be many more moths than butterflies visiting your garden. However, moths mostly fly by night and a good proportion of them are small and uninspiring from a distance, so we tend to pay them less attention. They also hide or camouflage themselves during the day with astonishing efficiency, choosing a surface that matches their patterns perfectly and resting quite motionless on it – which of course protects them from predators as well as curious humans. One very distinctive moth that flies during the day is the hummingbird hawkmoth, usually seen as a whir of orange wings and a greyish body, hovering over a flower. Look carefully and you may see it insert its long proboscis into tubular flowers, such as those of red valerian. This moth is a migrant, but several other hawkmoths are resident,

such as the privet hawkmoth and the elephant hawkmoth – an exotic-looking pink beauty that may visit honeysuckle on summer evenings.

A well-illustrated book is essential for identifying moths: there are over 2,000 British species and many of them are quite common. Some are much easier to identify than others, and this applies to both adults and larvae – most caterpillars that turn up in your garden will be moths of one sort or another. An adult moth that is easy to distinguish is the black-and-white magpie moth, which may be attracted to house lights. Its caterpillars eat the leaves of various garden plants including currants, gooseberries, heather and blackthorn. Equally wide-ranging in its choice of food plants is the prettily marked moth called the angle shades. One of the most striking is undoubtedly the sycamore moth caterpillar (*see* right). Getting to know moths opens up a whole world of fascinating detail, and you'll be surprised how many different kinds an ordinary garden can support.

Hummingbird hawkmoth

Elephant hawkmoth

Angle shades

Sycamore moth caterpillar

Mottled pug and smoky wainscot

Perhaps because they are so numerous, many insect species have no English name and can be identified only with a mind-bending concoction of Latin. Moths, however, are a rather memorable exception. Not only do many of them have English names, but the names themselves often make colourful reading. For example, common garden moths include the heart and dart; the mottled pug; the setaceous Hebrew character and the smoky wainscot. Many are graphically descriptive of the moth itself, making them easier to remember. The large yellow underwing is one of the commonest of these; the bloodvein, the yellow-tail, the dot moth, the shuttle-shaped dart and the white ermine are also fairly self-explanatory. And don't mistake the brown-line bright-eye for the bright-line brown-eye!

Encouraging beneficial insects

You might suppose that the insects in your garden fall neatly into two camps: bad (the ones that eat your plants) and good (the ones that eat the bad guys). Of course, things aren't that simple, and there is a whole complex web of interdependent relationships involving garden plant life and the hordes of small creatures that depend on it. Nevertheless, there are a few fairly common insects that help gardeners in various ways – chiefly pest control and pollination – and it's worth doing what you can to boost the populations of these invaluable visitors to your garden.

Pollination

Many garden crops need pollinating insects in order to produce fruit and seeds. Pollen has to be transferred from the male to the female parts of the flower – often within the same flower, sometimes in different flowers on the same plant, and sometimes from one plant to another. Certain insects, such as bees and butterflies, readily perform this valuable service, either because they are attracted to the pollen itself, or because they love nectar, the sweet liquid that many flowers contain. The nectar is usually cunningly located in the flower so that insects that are drawn to it have to pick up some pollen too – on the way in or out– which they then 'accidentally' transfer to the next flower they visit.

More ingenious still are some of the adaptations that help ensure that insects pollinate the right flowers. After all, it would be a waste for a bean plant to pollinate, say, a raspberry. Insects have differently structured mouthparts adapted to their particular method of feeding, such as sucking, chewing or biting. Nectar-feeding insects have a tongue or proboscis to suck up nectar, and the length of this varies – and so does the accessibility of nectar in different flowers. So hoverflies, which have short tongues, pollinate flat, open flowers such as poppies, while some

butterflies and moths, such as the hummingbird hawkmoth, have a very long proboscis to reach the nectar at the base of long, narrow flower tubes. Other clever adaptations exist: for example, only heavy insects like bumblebees can exert enough power to open the lip of a snapdragon.

For the gardener, arranging a variety of pollen and nectar supplies for insects is a pleasure – all you need to do is plant a varied assortment of old-fashioned flowers in a sunny place. Try to ensure continuity of supply by including plants that flower over a long period, such as red valerian and catmint, as well as those that will extend the nectar season – from hellebores, lungworts and crocuses that bloom in early spring right through to verbenas, Michaelmas daisies and sedums in autumn.

Various pollinating insects are suited to taking nectar from flowers that are differently structured.

① Different bumblebee species are adapted to different plants.

② Hoverflies have short tongues so flat, open flowers are best for them.

③ Hummingbird hawkmoths can reach nectar deep inside flower tubes.

Ten flowers to attract hoverflies

- Wild carrot (*Daucus carota*)
- *Eupatorium*
- Fennel (*Foeniculum vulgare*)
- Ox-eye daisy (*Leucanthemum vulgare*)
- Poached-egg flower (*Limnanthes douglasii*)
- Evening primrose (*Oenothera biennis*)
- Poppy (*Papaver*)
- Ice plant (*Sedum spectabile*)
- Golden rod (*Solidago*)
- Mullein (*Verbascum*)

Pest control

There are a few quite common insects that have a healthy appetite for some of the most irritating and common garden pests. Aphids such as greenfly and blackfly, which damage roses, broad beans, cherry trees and many other plants by sucking their sap, have soft bodies that even relatively small insects love to feast on. The larvae of hoverflies, ladybirds and lacewings (*see* pages 97–8) can all be counted upon to dispatch large numbers of aphids.

Hoverflies are among the easiest aphid-eaters to attract into a garden and the way to entice parent hoverflies into using your garden as a nursery is to lure them in with nectar. Many common garden flowers fit the bill. The female hoverfly will soon find an aphid-infested plant and lay her eggs, each of which will hatch into a legless larva. Aphid supplies in the garden will continue to sustain the hungry larvae – each of them will get through several hundred aphids, leaving only the desiccated skins.

Ideal hideaways

Ladybirds (*see* page 98) find their way into most gardens, and the best thing you can do to look after them is to make sure they have somewhere safe to shelter in winter. Hedges, shrubs, leaf litter and the hollow stems of last year's plants all offer dry nooks and crannies

that will see a ladybird through cold weather. Provided you aren't overly tidy, the ladybirds will be ready to emerge in spring and launch their young on your unsuspecting aphids.

Other insects that help gardeners by feeding on plant-eating pests include ants, wasps, spiders and certain beetles, such as the violet ground

beetle. As with ladybirds, make sure these small creatures and others like them have places to shelter, as well as overwinter, undisturbed, and they'll be there when you need them to feast on the bad guys. And remember that pesticides harm predator and prey alike, so don't be tempted to upset the balance by spraying.

Varied food and accommodation are key to attracting a range of garden-friendly insects.

① What ladybird, centipede or spider could resist a bijou residence like this attractively built shelter?

② Here, plants provide nectar, while a log pile offers basking surfaces as well as crevices for invertebrates to hide in.

Challenging sites

We've all seen magazine photos of joyous gardeners beaming over a plot that's perfect in every way, but you don't seem to meet them very often in real life. The real stars are the canny gardeners who know the limitations of their windy site, or frost pocket, or clay soil, and have learned how to make the best of it. With wildlife gardening just as with any other sort, choosing the right plants for your garden's site and soil can make a big difference.

Gardening against the odds

Despite what a disgruntled gardener may tell you, there are very few gardens where nothing will grow. Nature abhors a vacuum, and even really inhospitable places can develop well-adapted natural plant communities. Some great gardens have been made on incredibly difficult sites, from chalk pits to windswept cliff tops. There's no reason not to attempt a wildlife garden in unpromising circumstances. You just need to understand the ground rules and work with them.

Personal plant palette

Once you have put together a selection of plants that you hope will be your allies, there's no substitute for finding out for yourself which ones you can trust to thrive in your own particular conditions. A steady process of trial and error will help you to build up your own bespoke palette of tried-and-tested plants to use for different purposes: ground cover, structure, silver foliage, early flowers, late-season interest and nectar, long-lasting seedheads and berries for birds, and so on. You may be able to propagate these trusty plants and then use them again and again, either alongside newer acquisitions or as companions for others that might seem a little risky for your site. But don't imagine the old faithfuls will look boring. On the contrary, they will give valuable coherence to your planting and will

flatter all sorts of other plants in different ways. Best of all, you'll get to know them really well and can rely on them not to let you down.

Alliums are easy to grow, and loved by bees. *Allium sphaerocephalon* is a resilient one for late summer, here with variegated marjoram and phlox.

All-round survivors

Some plants just seem to be born survivors, putting up with a certain amount of harsh treatment and neglect, and coming back each year for more. Some may be a little tricky to establish in difficult conditions, but once you've got them going the chances are they will stick by you through thick and thin. Plants in this useful category that fit well into a wildlife garden include:

Bear's breeches (*Acanthus*)

Allium

Japanese anemone (*Anemone × hybrida*)

Hart's-tongue fern (*Asplenium scolopendrium*)

Perennial cornflower (*Centaurea montana*)

Red valerian (*Centranthus ruber*)

Dogwood (*Cornus alba*)

Cotoneaster horizontalis

Teasel (*Dipsacus fullonum*)

Leopard's bane (*Doronicum*)

Globe thistle (*Echinops*)

Sea daisy (*Erigeron karvinskianus*)

Miss Willmott's ghost (*Eryngium giganteum*)

Eupatorium

Euphorbia amygdaloides var. *robbiae*

Geranium × magnificum

Stinking iris (*Iris foetidissima*)

Winter jasmine (*Jasminum nudiflorum*)

Summer snowflake (*Leucojum aestivum*)

Oriental poppy (*Papaver orientale*)

Bistort (*Persicaria bistorta* 'Superba')

Phlomis fruticosa

Rosa rugosa

Christmas box (*Sarcococca confusa*)

Town and city gardens

Making a wildlife garden in the heart of town may seem like a tall order, but most cities contain far more wildlife than you think, so your visitors may not have far to travel. Gardens play an important role in the whole urban network of green spaces, acting as links between the city's different habitats.

Urban wildlife

Initiatives to bring wildlife and all its benefits into towns are increasing all the time. Flowering meadows are beginning to be seen in some city parks in place of mown grass, and installing living walls and green roofs (*see* page 49) is a growing trend.

City farms are thriving, and many schools have nature gardens. Groups of 'guerrilla gardeners', too, create pockets of wildlife habitat when they transform dead or neglected spaces, such as traffic islands, into gardens.

In addition to public parks and gardens, wild creatures take

advantage of waste land and derelict buildings as well as the valuable 'wildlife corridors' created by railways and canals where land is seldom disturbed. Bramble-covered embankments offer homes for urban foxes and provide abundant food for birds and butterflies.

How gardens fit in

Enticing wildlife into your city garden starts with seeing your patch as part of a whole. Planting trees and hedges will help to link wildlife hotspots, giving birds, animals and insects safe cover to move around in their search for food and breeding places. Climbers like honeysuckle, jasmine and ivy provide nesting places without taking up much garden space, as do wall shrubs. A small water feature or a bird bath is a must, and planting nectar-rich flowers will help sustain urban bees and other insects. Many towns have thriving groups of beekeepers, and if you have space you might even consider having a hive yourself. (*See also* pages 34–5 and 49 for wildlife where space is limited.)

Varied, nectar-rich planting has transformed this small garden into a haven for London-dwelling bees and butterflies (and people, too).

New gardens

Don't be daunted by the prospect of creating a wildlife garden from scratch. It's true, of course, that some wildlife habitats such as woodland and mature hedges take years to develop, but wild creatures know a good opportunity when they see one. A surprising number of them won't be slow to move in if you provide accommodation and a varied food supply.

First steps

Having a blank canvas allows you to plan and plant up your garden from the outset, and hopefully get everything in the right place without having to work round existing features. Try to get a mixed native hedge in somewhere if you can (*see* pages 32–3). Also, take a little time to find the right location for your choice of tree or trees, and put in a few fast-growing flowering shrubs. Buddleias, brooms (*Cytisus*), ornamental elders (*Sambucus nigra*), mahonias and ceanothus are all ideal to try for starters. Good-quality plants will make plenty of growth in their first year, soon providing some cover for birds and insects, as well as nectar to attract bees, butterflies

Buddleia and *Anthemis*: both are encouragingly quick to establish, and great together to entice butterflies, moths, bees and hoverflies into your new garden.

and hoverflies. Elders and buddleias also grow easily from cuttings, so you can increase your stock very cheaply. Plant densely to begin with; you can always remove or cut back some of these starter shrubs when other slower-growing plants have become established.

Filling the borders

Many perennials are also easy to propagate by splitting up clumps, so are good value in the first year or two. Some, such as *Eupatorium*, will bulk up and fill space quite quickly, and penstemons, mallows (*Lavatera*) and *Anthemis* usually get off to a flying start. You can supplement them by sowing seed of a range of

'fillers' – honesty, teasels, Miss Willmott's ghost (*Eryngium giganteum*), Welsh poppies, evening primrose, poached-egg flower (*Limnanthes douglasii*), foxgloves and forget-me-nots – that will probably self-sow once they are established. Or plant the huge, biennial, prickly Scotch thistle, *Onopordum acanthium*, for quick structure. It's also irresistible to bees and produces seed that finches enjoy in winter.

Enjoy your weeds

While you wait for your plants to establish, leave a small area fallow to see what turns up by itself. The seeds of many wildflowers, such as poppies, stay viable in the soil for many years and within just a few weeks you'll probably have a variety of flowering 'weeds' to bring in the insects.

Don't forget

Provide food and water for birds from day one. Your long-term aim will be to establish a self-sustaining wildlife community, but that takes time and you may as well put up the 'welcome' sign while you're waiting.

Boggy gardens

Making a conventional garden with lawns and beds on a very boggy site can be fraught with difficulty and involve creating raised areas or undertaking expensive drainage work. But damp ground is a tremendously valuable wildlife habitat, so stop worrying about the boggiest parts of your garden and welcome them as an opportunity to grow some of the many fantastic plants that are perfectly happy to have wet feet.

Trees and shrubs for moist soil

Trees that revel in damp conditions include native willows and alder. Both are brilliant trees for wildlife, if you have plenty of space in your damp garden and can plant them at a safe distance from your house and drains. Goat willow (*Salix caprea*), also known as pussy willow, is one of the best of all trees for insects. It attracts many moth species (some of whose larvae feed on the wood and others on the leaves) and is always alive with the hum of bees in early spring when its abundant catkins open. Alder (*Alnus glutinosa*) is also attractive early in the year, producing long, colourful catkins. In winter the seeds in its cones may attract siskins and redpolls.

Don't forget

In ground that gets very wet in winter, delay planting until early spring so that dormant plants do not have to sit around for months with waterlogged roots. Container-grown shrubs and herbaceous plants can be planted even later in the season.

Perennials for damp borders

Bugle (*Ajuga reptans*)
Water saxifrage (*Darmera peltata*)
Eupatorium
Siberian iris (*Iris sibirica*)
Ligularia
Lobelia
Loosestrife (*Lysimachia* and *Lythrum*)
Bistort (*Persicaria bistorta* 'Superba')
Giant cowslip (*Primula florindae*)
Meadow buttercup (*Ranunculus acris*)
Rodgersia
Bog sage (*Salvia uliginosa*)
Burnet (*Sanguisorba*)
Globeflower (*Trollius*)
Arum lily (*Zantedeschia aethiopica*)

Various willows can be grown as shrubs. Some, such as cultivars of the native white willow (*Salix alba*) and purple willow (*Salix purpurea*), have colourful bark on their young shoots. Coppice or pollard them every year in early spring and use the prunings to make attractive structures in living willow, such as an arbour, a play tunnel or an arch (*see* page 20).

Shrubs for wet places include quite a few 'wildings', such as guelder rose (*Viburnum opulus*) and elder (*Sambucus nigra*), and several garden favourites, including many of the viburnums, dogwoods (*Cornus alba*) and *Spiraea*, will tolerate a lot of water. The range of plants you can grow will increase if you work in plenty of grit and compost to help aerate and drain the soil.

Even a tiny patch of damp grass can achieve this lovely spring effect with snakeshead fritillaries and buttercups.

Dry gardens

A well-drained, sun-baked garden is just the thing for bees and butterflies. It offers ideal conditions for many of the nectar-rich plants they love best, such as aromatic herbs, many spring-flowering bulbs and succulents like sedums. Provided water is available in a pond or bird bath (or both), there's no reason why a dry garden shouldn't be a good place for wildlife.

Working with dry soil

Free-draining soils – usually sandy, gravelly or chalky – are easy to work and quick to warm up after winter. But gardening on dry soil has its challenges, namely establishing young plants and coping with prolonged droughts.

Working with the seasons and the weather will help to give your new plants the best start. Plant trees, shrubs and perennials in autumn so they can settle in when droughts aren't a threat, and mulch the soil in early spring before the surface dries out. Take advantage of damp spells for planting and sowing, and soak new plants in a bucket of water for an hour or so before planting. If you need to sow seeds in dry weather, water the drills first: this will help to keep conditions damp. Many hardy annuals can be sown in autumn, and should establish well over the winter while there's still plenty of moisture around. Plant wildflowers as plugs, either bought or raised by sowing your own seeds in modules. A plug plant well rooted into its compost is much more likely to shrug off a few dry days than a bare-root transplant.

Plant adaptations

Many plants in the wild survive drought because they have a number of adaptations that help them to retain moisture. Teasels, dandelions, fennel and wild carrot – all very attractive to hoverflies and other insects – have deep tap roots that store water to see them through periods when there's no rain. Other plants have hairs on their leaves: these act as a protective or reflective layer that stops them drying out. The giant Scotch thistle (*Onopordum acanthium*) and lamb's ears (*Stachys byzantina*) come into this category. Both are a favourite with bees. Waxy, leathery or succulent leaves, such as those of sedums, houseleeks and *Euphorbia myrsinites*, also prevent moisture loss. Many familiar spring bulbs flower while the soil is still damp, spending the dry months underground in a state of dormancy.

Plants for gravel

Agrimony (*Agrimonia eupatoria*)
Allium
Viper's bugloss (*Echium vulgare*)
Sea daisy (*Erigeron karvinskianus*)
Eryngium
Hawkweed (*Hieracium* or *Pilosella*)
Marjoram (*Origanum*)
Sisyrinchium striatum
Thyme (*Thymus*)
Goat's-beard (*Tragopogon pratensis*)
Verbena bonariensis

Don't forget

Gravel is a useful surface material in dry gardens, keeping the soil underneath surprisingly damp, even when the surface is baked by the sun. It lends itself to a variety of plants and planting styles (see above).

Beth Chatto's gravel garden in Essex is a shining example of how to plant beautifully on difficult, dry soil.

Windy gardens

A few plants seem to take being buffeted by the wind completely in their stride, but for most, wind can be punishing and slow down growth. An open, windswept site is also one of the most difficult for wildlife. Any shelter that you're able to create in an exposed area will reduce the force of the wind and is sure to be appreciated by both plants and wildlife.

This collection of ground-hugging plants, anchored in gravel, should stand up to the most brutal sea winds.

Wind-tolerant plants

Perennials that are native or widely naturalized near the coast are accustomed to sea breezes and will thrive in windy gardens without mollycoddling. Try sea holly (*Eryngium maritimum*), red valerian (*Centranthus ruber*), sea daisy (*Erigeron karvinskianus*), thrift (*Armeria maritima*), sea kale (*Crambe maritima*), crocosmias and sea lavender (*Limonium platyphyllum*).

Many grasses, too, suit windswept locations, swaying attractively in the breeze and providing shelter for insects among their stems. Choose quaking grass (*Briza media*) and foxtail barley (*Hordeum jubatum*) or the native coastal blue lyme-grass (*Leymus arenarius*) – though you will have to curb its tendency to run.

Creating shelter

Even a stout fence may not be the best kind of shelter for a very windy garden: solid fencing can create a lot of turbulence, so it may well get damaged or even blown down. A hedge or shelter belt can be tricky to establish but will go from strength to strength as it matures, and will filter the wind much more satisfactorily. Choose a mixture of tough native plants such as hawthorn (*Crataegus monogyna*), willow (*Salix*), guelder rose (*Viburnum opulus*), sea buckthorn (*Hippophae rhamnoides*) and blackthorn (*Prunus spinosa*) for areas exposed to cold easterly or northerly winds. If you want a small tree in an exposed position, hawthorn is hard to beat. Tough to the core, it produces blossom and berries to give two seasons of interest for you and for your garden wildlife.

Shady gardens

Shade, at least some of the time, suits many creatures perfectly, making them less conspicuous and helping them to keep cool and damp in dry weather. And there are a great many plants that tolerate and even prefer shade, whether damp or dry. Aim to lighten up areas of dense shade if you can, so you can grow flowers and attract nectar-seeking insects into your garden.

Creating dappled shade

A pair of secateurs and a saw, judiciously applied, can make all the difference to a shady garden. Thinning or raising the canopy of a tree or shrub can create attractive dappled shade in summer, dispelling the gloom beneath. Pruning large trees is best left to the professionals, and may be expensive, but if a little-used dark space is transformed into a pretty woodland garden it will have been worth it.

Shade in gardens is often created unintentionally when a tree or shrub outgrows its space and eventually becomes a light-excluding monster. So think very carefully when you choose trees for the garden, and do your homework. Rowans and birches, for example, have a light canopy that will never cast deep shade, and they're both excellent for wildlife. Coppiced hazel (*see* page 25) will create a woodland effect without ever getting unmanageable, and it also gives woodland birds, insects and wildflowers the conditions they need to flourish.

Make clearings in shady areas to plant foxgloves. The white ones look really striking against a dark background.

Plants for deep shade

Most plants won't thrive in sunless spots at the base of a north-facing wall or fence, or under an evergreen tree or hedge, because they are likely to have to put up with dryness as well as shade. But before you give up, here are a few long-suffering, last-resort plants that may at least provide some greenery in those places where you think nothing will grow:

Marbled arum (*Arum italicum* subsp. *italicum* 'Marmoratum')

Asarabacca (*Asarum europaeum*)

Hart's-tongue fern (*Asplenium scolopendrium*)

Cyclamen (*Cyclamen hederifolium*)

Spurge laurel (*Daphne laureola*)

Wood spurge (*Euphorbia amygdaloides*)

Common ivy (*Hedera helix*)

Stinking iris (*Iris foetidissima*)

Greater woodrush (*Luzula sylvatica*)

Polypody fern (*Polypodium vulgare*)

Soft shield fern (*Polystichum setiferum*)

Butcher's broom (*Ruscus aculeatus*)

Don't forget

Pale flowers such as white periwinkle, foxgloves or honesty show up much better in partial shade. For the prettiest effects, choose a mixture with different shapes and textures. Try a combination of sweet woodruff (*Galium odoratum*), sweet Cicely (*Myrrhis odorata*) and Solomon's seal (*Polygonatum* x *hybridum*).

The native hart's-tongue fern flatters many other shade-lovers such as hostas, and is a tough and easy plant.

Chalky soil

Shallow, chalky soil can make for frustrating gardening. It's often full of flints, and dries out almost instantly in sunny weather. Vegetables, roses and anything else that needs a lot of nourishment may struggle. However, plenty of other plants are perfectly well adapted to thin, alkaline soil, including many native wildflowers that are attractive to butterflies. With a little care in the early stages, it needn't be difficult to establish a varied planting scheme.

These plants are well kitted out to cope with dry, chalky soil: sedums store water in their succulent leaves, fennel in its deep tap root.

Wild plants of chalk and limestone

Some of the richest wild plant communities are found in unimproved chalk downland, partly because the poor soil makes it difficult for aggressive plants and vigorous grasses to compete and overwhelm them. Gardens with chalky soil are, therefore, good places to try and establish a flowering meadow with wildflowers that will adapt and thrive. These include cowslips (*Primula veris*), bloody cranesbill (*Geranium sanguineum*), Pasque flower (*Pulsatilla vulgaris*), wild marjoram (*Origanum vulgare*) and clustered bellflower (*Campanula glomerata*). Wildflower suppliers even sell some downland orchids, such as pyramidal and fragrant orchids (though their success is by no means guaranteed). As with all plants, do make sure they have been sourced responsibly and not dug up from the wild.

Many varieties of clematis (the wild form, *Clematis vitalba*, is the familiar, rampant old man's beard of chalkland) will grow happily on chalky soils as long as their roots have some moisture. And there are several wildlife-friendly shrubs that are native to chalk and limestone regions including spindle (*Euonymus europaeus*), box (*Buxus sempervirens*), juniper (*Juniperus communis*), blackthorn (*Prunus spinosa*) and buckthorn (*Rhamnus cathartica*).

Improving chalky soil

Adding organic matter to the soil on a regular basis is the only way to grow a wide range of plants in chalky areas. But you will need a lot of it because these hungry soils rapidly mop up all the compost, leaf mould and manure you can get hold of. Alkaline soils tend to be rich in bacteria and worms, which get busy as soon as you dig in any humus and break it down very quickly.

Border flowers for chalky soil

Knapweed (*Centaurea*)
Red valerian (*Centranthus ruber*)
Wallflower (*Erysimum*)
Euphorbia
Hellebore (*Helleborus*)
Catmint (*Nepeta*)
Oriental poppy (*Papaver orientale*)
Scabious (*Scabiosa*)
Sedum
Sisyrinchium
Mullein (*Verbascum*)

Don't forget

Help prevent evaporation from the surface of dry, chalky soil by planting mat-forming perennials as a covering. Plant hardy geraniums and sedums in sunny places, and try sweet woodruff (*Galium odoratum*), dead nettle (*Lamium*) and *Epimedium* in the shade. They'll give cover for insects and small mammals, and help suppress weeds too.

Acid soil

Sometimes envied by gardeners because they suit some of the most cherished exotics – such as rhododendrons, camellias, Japanese maples and magnolias – acid soils do vary. They can consist of peat, sand or clay, and what grows best will depend on how moisture-retentive your particular soil is.

Bee-friendly shrubs

A number of acid-loving plants are well worth their space in a wildlife garden because they are attractive to bees. Heather honey is much prized: bees love wild heather (*Calluna vulgaris*), known as ling, which must have acid soil. They are also equally fond of the less fussy winter-flowering kinds, which are mostly heaths (*Erica*). With their long flowering season, these plants are a lifeline for bumblebees on sunny days in winter and early spring. Heathers have succeeded so well in the wild partly because they are unpalatable to herbivores.

Witch hazels (*Hamamelis*) and the graceful early-spring shrub *Corylopsis pauciflora* are both valuable sources of unseasonal nectar. They are followed by skimmias, some of which have wonderfully scented spring blossom and others very long-lasting berries, provided you grow both male and female forms. The hybrid called 'Kew Green' is a good pollinator for berrying females, and also very fragrant. Free-draining sandy soils that are not excessively

Flowering heathers and heaths

Calluna vulgaris 'Blazeaway' (lilac)

Calluna vulgaris 'Silver Knight' (mauve)

Calluna vulgaris 'Spring Torch' (purple)

Erica arborea var. *alpina* (white)

Erica carnea 'Myretoun Ruby' (rose pink)

Erica carnea 'Rosalie' (bright pink)

Erica carnea f. *alba* 'Springwood White' (white)

Erica × *darleyensis* 'Darley Dale' (shell pink)

acid are ideal for brooms. There are many varieties, flowering in late spring and early summer.

In late summer, the magnetic effect on bees of the choice white-flowered shrub *Eucryphia*, and the similar honey-scented *Hoheria*, must be seen to be believed. These are most likely to succeed on humus-rich acid to neutral soil.

Winter nectar for insects would be reason enough to grow witch hazels, but the charming little flowers lift our spirits at a dreary time of year, too.

Season by season

We may grumble about the vagaries of the weather, but who would be without the changing seasons and the range of experiences they bring? And with its cycles of new growth, migration, breeding and surviving the winter, wildlife is as varied and exciting through the year as anything in the garden. If you bear the seasons in mind when choosing plants you'll ensure there's always something new and interesting, and both you and your garden wildlife will benefit.

Wildlife through the year

The most successful wildlife gardeners make a commitment to supply their garden visitors with what they need at each season of the year. But it isn't quite like looking after pets or farm animals. If you set them up with the habitat that suits them, wild creatures will just get on with it, feeding, breeding and generally living out their lives without constant interference from you. Plan and plant your garden with their seasonal requirements broadly in mind, and you'll be at least halfway there.

The arrival of cuckoos has long been a special sign of spring. In recent years, declining numbers have made their familiar call more of a rarity.

From this point, it only remains to anticipate what your visitors need and when, and offer help when it's needed. Sometimes they'll do just fine without you. But if you keep in touch with the annual cycles of comings and goings, get to know the behaviour patterns of birds and animals, and follow changes in the weather, you'll know when to intervene. The most obvious offerings – extra food when it's cold or when parent birds are feeding babies, extra water when it's dry or frosty – can make all the difference.

Travellers from afar

Seasonal migration is one of the most fascinating aspects of the natural world's annual cycle. It's extraordinary that we should be able to welcome into our gardens a tiny creature that has just flown hundreds or even thousands of miles (in some cases without even stopping to rest). Fieldfares and redwings may arrive in our hedgerows in autumn. They come here to escape the colder winters of their breeding grounds, in Scandinavia and northern Europe. Our most familiar migrants – swifts, swallows, martins and the majority of warblers – spend the winters in warmer climates around the Mediterranean or in Africa and move north in spring to breed in Britain. Amazingly, some of our garden insects may have travelled just as far. They include painted lady and red admiral butterflies, and certain moths, such as the hummingbird hawkmoth and the silver Y.

Climate change is causing some worrying alterations in migration trends. Willow warblers, cuckoos and other birds whose annual journey includes crossing desert areas of Africa are struggling. As these arid areas expand, it makes the difficult part of the birds' route even longer. Blackcaps and chiffchaffs now regularly overwinter in Britain, as do red admirals, although some of these will perish if the weather turns really cold.

The most urgent need of newly arrived migrants is food. A garden with a good insect population will help restore exhausted warblers, while apples on the ground, or a yew tree laden with berries, may appeal to fieldfares in cold weather. Summer migrants also need nesting places (*see* pages 46–8).

Pyracantha berries go down well with blackbirds, and the midsummer blossom is always alive with bees.

Spring

Most people have a favourite time of year, and for many of us spring is the clear winner. Watching your garden come to life a bit more each day after the winter always seems miraculous, and it's even more absorbing if you take an interest in the creatures that share your patch. Birdsong and sunshine are back; the days are lengthening, woodland wildflowers are at their best and wherever you look there are blossoming trees and fresh greenery.

Young blackbirds are among the most familiar and characterful baby birds in the garden. You'll often hear them squawking for food as they trail after their industrious parents.

Site nest boxes among foliage to give them cover, but make sure it isn't easy for cats to climb up and gain access.

birds to conceal their nests from predators in the weeks before trees and hedges have their full covering of leaves. Include some evergreens among your garden shrubs and climbers and you'll help to provide safe cover for early birds.

Spring is a magical time in woodland as it progresses from bare branches to a full canopy of leaves. Woodland wildflowers are adapted to spring sunshine and summer shade, and it's easy to capture a similar effect in the garden, using trees, shrubs or even a deciduous hedge, with bulbs and perennials beneath (*see* pages 24–5). The mixture of plant types and of light conditions make a rich and varied habitat that suits a wide range of creatures from beetles and butterflies to woodland birds.

Early birds and flowers

Spring highlights are many, but the first sight of a bird gathering nesting material is always exciting. The earliest to begin breeding are usually blackbirds, robins and other resident birds. By starting in the first mild spell of the year, they improve their chances of being able to raise two or more successive broods. Early nesters do, however, run the risk of capricious weather, and food shortages if cold days and nights mean insect populations are slow to build up. It's also more difficult for

Tips and tasks for spring

Finish tidying borders before the rush of spring growth begins. Cut down the last of the seedheads: they

The soundtrack to spring

Some birds, such as robins, can be heard in almost any month of the year, but spring is the season we most associate with birdsong. At this time of year male birds, which do most or all of the singing, are starting to defend a territory and/or attract a mate. Hearing the first cuckoo is a classic rite of spring, though, like many migrant birds, cuckoos are in decline and they are heard less often. But spring is heralded by the calls of the really 'early birds', such as great tits and chiffchaffs; their easily recognized two-note calls accompany late-winter sunshine. The first chatterings of passing swallows can be heard a few weeks later. Melodies come courtesy of blackbirds, thrushes, chaffinches and blackcaps among others, while dunnocks and the tiny wren punch above their weight with their explosive little songs. Once you have fixed a bird's song in your mind, you'll remember it always. Try to learn a couple of new ones each year, and you will soon get to know which birds are around in your neighbourhood.

Don't forget

Do keep feeding garden birds. They have a lot of energetic work to do in the breeding season, and wild food can be scarce in dry or cold spells. Aim to provide supplementary food for parent birds, leaving them free to concentrate on finding the more specialized and nutritious foods that their chicks need.

begin to look out of place amid the returning greenery – and save any remaining seeds to sow elsewhere. Spread a mulch of compost when the ground is damp, to help rejuvenate the soil and retain moisture. But be careful when you excavate the compost heap in case it is home to hibernating hedgehogs or slow-worms.

Each year, lift a clump or two of snowdrops when flowering is over, and split them into individual bulbs to replant elsewhere or give to friends. Choose a damp day in late spring to lift and divide clumps of

Don't forget

Make time to appreciate all those special moments in the spring wildlife garden. Smell the fragrance of cherry, pear or apple blossom on a warm day; listen to the dawn chorus, or a thrush singing out the last of the evening twilight. Watch newly emerged queen bees collecting nectar in the sunshine. It will be a whole 12 months before the opportunity comes round again!

primroses and violets that have finished flowering, or to transplant self-sown hellebore seedlings.

Watch out for early appearances from unwelcome insects such as vine weevils and lily beetles. If you take steps to control their numbers early in the year, they will not reproduce as rapidly. The same goes for slugs and snails: a torchlight slug-hunting expedition on a mild, damp, spring night not only saves vulnerable young plants now, but also means you won't have their offspring to contend with later in the year. One kind of early insect that you don't usually need to worry about when it appears each spring is the froghopper, a small sap-sucking bug that is conspicuous only because it covers itself with a white froth (known as 'cuckoo spit') produced by its larvae.

Now is a good time to spread all that lovely compost you've been making and give a boost to flowering plants.

Nectar plants for early spring

Bugle (*Ajuga reptans*)
Cuckoo flower (*Cardamine pratensis*)
Crocus 'Snow Bunting'
Hellebore (*Helleborus*)
Honesty (*Lunaria annua*)
Primrose (*Primula vulgaris*)
Cherry plum (*Prunus cerasifera*)
Blackthorn (*Prunus spinosa*)
Goat willow (*Salix caprea*)
Sweet violet (*Viola odorata*)

Primroses, hellebores and other woodland plants, in all their variety, make a great show before trees come into leaf, and are good for early bees.

Summer

For many of us, the summer garden is all about enjoying the sunshine and flowers. It's the same for butterflies, bees, moths and the many flies and bugs that are attracted to nectar and pollen. From roses and lavender to hollyhocks and Michaelmas daisies, the garden's insect population is spoilt for choice for weeks on end, as flowers come and go in the main floral extravaganza of the gardening year.

Swallows are among the most graceful of pest-control operatives, each pair needing thousands of insects to feed their growing brood.

Watering wisely

Few gardens will get through a summer without some additional water. Light showers don't usually provide nearly enough, so unless there has been a heavy downpour or a long period of steady rain, be on the alert for plants showing signs of distress, especially those that are about to flower. In dry periods, young trees and shrubs can be very vulnerable so give them priority when watering. And – just as important – make sure birds don't run out of water either. Refill bird baths every day, and keep an eye on the level of the pond, topping up with rainwater from a water butt when necessary.

Keeping the soil covered with vegetation is especially important in summer, not only to help control weeds and prevent evaporation but also to provide shade and shelter for the many creatures, for instance frogs and earthworms, that dislike dry heat. If you cut back plants such as hardy geraniums and lady's mantle (*Alchemilla mollis*) after flowering, they will grow a mound

Cut back lady's mantle for a new crop of leaves. Dew and rain cling to them, attracting thirsty insects.

Birds love water, especially in hot weather, so keep your bird bath regularly topped up.

Ants and their colonies

Like many insects, ants can undoubtedly be irritating when you're having a picnic outside, or if they appear in the greenhouse or infest a potted plant. Yet many of the colonies of black, yellow or red ants found in gardens do no real harm, living their lives beneath paving stones, in compost heaps or under turf (which they can help to aerate). As well as your sandwiches, ants like to eat certain other insects and are a useful indicator of aphid infestations: they 'milk' aphids for their sweet honeydew, and can often be seen marching up plant stems towards their sticky target.

Like bees and wasps, ants live in complex social colonies consisting of a queen, whose job is to lay eggs, and many smaller workers who build the nest, gather food and generally keep the show on the road. The nest consists of an arrangement of passageways and chambers excavated in the soil. Some of these are used for incubating and hatching the eggs, which the workers carry there from the queen's central chamber. The queen ants may live for several years. The notorious 'marriage flights' of ant colonies, usually in late summer, can be bothersome but many of the ants involved – future queens and the males that hope to mate with them – are soon gobbled up by delighted birds.

of new foliage that makes useful ground cover for the rest of the season and also helps to keep things looking fresh. Compact evergreen shrubs will help, too.

Tips and tasks for summer

Birds with young to feed should be a big help with many potential pest problems, but watch those cabbage plants for caterpillars of the large white and small white butterflies. They will quickly reduce the leaves to lacework if neither you nor the birds get to them in time. Pick caterpillars off by hand or go for the labour-saving option and cover the plants with fine netting when you plant them out. This will keep the butterflies off as long as you ensure there are no small holes or gaps.

Dry summer days offer a good opportunity to collect seeds of wildflowers such as cowslips, foxgloves, columbines, poppies and yellow rattle, to increase your own stock or give away. It's easier to scatter the seeds straightaway, and fresh seeds often have a better germination rate. Alternatively, clean off the chaff, remove any creepy-

Foxgloves, alliums and catmint are easy, wildlife-friendly plants for the early-summer border. After flowering, cut the catmint back so it will bloom again; also scatter foxglove seeds.

Plants for evening

Even if they happen rarely, those fragrant, balmy evenings of high summer are special enough to be worth planning for. Choose plants that both you and your garden's moth population (undoubtedly larger than you may imagine) will enjoy, such as honeysuckle, jasmine and phlox, not forgetting evening primroses, and annuals raised from seed, for example tobacco plants (*Nicotiana sylvestris*), night-scented stocks (*Matthiola bicornis*) and petunias (especially the purple ones, which are usually the most fragrant).

Don't forget

Take photographs or make a note of plants that bees, butterflies and hoverflies enjoy. As well as the ones recommended in books, you may well notice other plants that they find irresistible. You can then increase your stock of the most popular specimens by saving seed, taking cuttings or dividing the plants at the appropriate time of year.

crawlies, and store the seeds in labelled paper envelopes in a cool, dark, dry place for sowing in autumn or next spring.

Late summer is a good time to cut hedges: there's little risk then of disturbing nesting birds (but do check first), and the new growth will have a chance to toughen up before cold weather begins. Another job for late summer is to thin out pond growth, removing excess waterweed and the older leaves of plants that have outgrown their space.

Autumn

When late summer passes into early autumn, it's a tranquil time in the wildlife garden. With the breeding season over, young birds and animals have been launched into independent living, and many adult birds seem to be absent: they stay hidden and quiet to shed and regrow their feathers and to recover from the hard work of raising a family. Natural food is plentiful, with seeds, berries and insects all readily available. But the first chilly nights of autumn are a timely reminder that many creatures are going to need our help in the lean months to come.

Spiders' webs are useful for catching pests and look beautiful when they catch the low autumn light.

Seeds and berries

The autumn garden can be a real joy if the weather is kind. Growth slows down so that routine maintenance seems less urgent, and the low, golden light emphasizes the shapes and colours of plants. Architectural seedheads such as teasels (*Dipsacus fullonum*) and the durable, neat tiers of *Phlomis russeliana* look wonderful in the morning sunshine, festooned with dew-spangled spiders' webs.

Seed-eating birds, particularly chaffinches and goldfinches, like to probe the spent flowerheads of such plants for food. And when the seeds have all gone, the plant's sturdy skeleton makes a wonderful structural feature, especially when decorated with snow or hoar frost. Seedheads that won't last all winter can be left until they collapse and look bedraggled – usually in the first wet, cold spell.

Other birds prefer their seeds wrapped in something tasty. Berries and fruits of all kinds and colours provide sustenance for them, and sometimes for us too. It's hard to decide how much space to give to those that the birds like to eat (cotoneaster and pyracantha), as opposed to those that we prefer (apples and figs). And then there are those berries that neither humans nor birds are very keen on but will look handsome for a few months. Planting a few of each is usually the best solution, and there should be something left on the bushes in late winter to help birds survive if they get really hungry. (*See also* pages 64–5 and 74–5.)

Don't be in a hurry to cut down seedheads. Sedums can look good all winter; others provide autumn food and shelter for birds and insects.

Tips and tasks for autumn

Take care to include in your borders some plants that will keep the nectar supply going in autumn for late-season butterflies and bees. There's a useful late-flowering *Buddleja davidii* called 'Autumn Beauty' (which may be hard to find) or try *Escallonia bifida* or the shrubby ivy *Hedera helix* 'Arborescens'. Provided it isn't damaging any structures, any mature, flowering ivy is useful both for its unusually late, nectar-bearing flowers and for its black berries, which will sustain desperately hungry birds in midwinter.

When you buy your spring bulbs in early autumn, spare a thought for any wild areas of the garden. Species crocuses, dwarf daffodils, squills (*Scilla*), wood anemones (*Anemone blanda*) and glory of the snow (*Chionodoxa*) are all ideal for growing in grass, providing nectar for

Don't let dead leaves smother your grass for too long. Rake them up and stack them to make leaf mould.

A log pile makes a snug shelter for beetles, centipedes, spiders and other helpful mini-beasts.

Social wasps

If, one day in autumn, you suddenly notice the absence of wasps, it isn't just because it has dawned on them that the season for al fresco meals is over. Our most familiar wasps are social insects and, like bumblebees and ants, they build up short-lived colonies in the summer months. Nearly all of them die off in autumn, leaving only the newly mated females – the queens. These (much larger) queen wasps and bees hibernate, then emerge after the winter and search for a place to begin building an intricate new nest.

Don't forget

Late autumn is often the best time to plant bare-root deciduous trees, shrubs and hedging. Provided the winter is not too harsh, their roots will be able to establish and get plenty of water before having to cope with any periods of drought. When the weather warms up in spring, the plants should grow away.

emerging bees in early spring and fading away after flowering without leaving tangles of dying foliage. Buy twice as many as you think you need: they won't break the bank, and you're sure to find lots of places to plant them. Most multiply well in time, and when they flower you'll be thankful you planted generously.

If you have a fruiting tree, you'll no doubt store your own freshly picked, undamaged apples in trays stacked in a garage or well-insulated shed. Put out any surplus fruit, especially if it is starting to go soft, for blackbirds and thrushes on the coldest days of winter. Migrant fieldfares and redwings may come and join the feast, too.

Bear in mind the creatures that are preparing to hibernate (*see* pages 122–3) and don't tidy away all the debris that might give them a place to call their own for the winter. Heaps of fallen leaves in odd corners needn't be unsightly, and a log pile can be neatly stacked and still provide shelter for beetles and frogs. However, it's worth giving the grass a final cut on a fine, dry day in late autumn. Early spring bulbs always look so much better if the grass around them is green and neat.

Winter

With many plants and animals dormant, winter is the season of rest – for gardeners and for much of the natural world. During these cold, dark months we notice and appreciate winter plants like snowdrops and hellebores, simply because flowers are more of a rarity. For the same reason, winter is often the best time to observe and connect with those creatures that are still active in the garden.

Keep an eye open for fieldfares, especially in very cold weather when they may visit gardens for windfall apples and berries such as cotoneaster (shown here) and yew.

Looking after the birds

Birds are leading players in the garden wildlife cast all year, but in winter they really take centre stage as they get hungrier and come to rely on us for food. Watching them from the window is one of winter's great pleasures. Bird tables and feeders, as well as the plant food found in gardens, undoubtedly save lives in cold weather, and once birds are in the habit of visiting you regularly it's important to keep up the supply. For this reason, it's always worth growing an assortment of plants that bear winter berries (*see* pages 64–5).

In very cold or snowy spells, birds that don't usually visit may arrive in search of food and shelter. These can include bramblings, siskins, reed buntings, fieldfares, moorhens and occasionally even flocks of exotic-looking waxwings. Gardens and the food they provide are thought to be a factor in the increasing number of formerly migratory birds that now overwinter in Britain, such as blackcaps and chiffchaffs.

Hibernation

Quite a few mammals, such as rabbits and most mice and squirrels, stay active throughout the winter if they can find enough food to keep their systems running and stay warm. Many, however, will tuck themselves away to conserve energy

Helping ladybirds through winter will mean fewer aphids in late spring, when ladybird larvae begin to eat them.

Evergreens for winter cover

Common ivy (*Hedera helix,* shown below)
Holly (*Ilex aquifolium*)
Greater woodrush (*Luzula sylvatica*)
Polypody fern (*Polypodium vulgare*)
Soft shield fern (*Polystichum setiferum*)
Butcher's broom (*Ruscus aculeatus*)
Yew (*Taxus baccata*)

Don't forget

Keeping bird feeders well stocked all winter not only helps the birds, but also encourages them to explore other parts of your garden. They will search nooks and crannies for overwintering slugs, caterpillars and other larvae that might otherwise be waiting to devour next year's vegetable and fruit crops.

in really severe weather. Other animals, including slow-worms, hedgehogs, bats and many insects, survive by 'shutting down'. They hide away in late autumn, their metabolic rate drops and they don't move or feed for several months. Winter accommodation needs vary greatly: slow-worms hibernate underground or in compost heaps; bats choose lofts or hollow trees; hedgehogs make a heap of dead leaves under a hedge or other protecting vegetation. Butterflies that hibernate as adults, such as the peacock and small tortoiseshell, may find a spot in a shed or in the house, perhaps emerging prematurely into a warm room. If that happens, move them very gently to somewhere that's cool and dark.

Tips and tasks for winter

Some of the most satisfying winter gardening jobs are the ones you carry out in anticipation of spring. You can put up new nest boxes to allow birds a chance to explore and get used to them, well before they need to start looking for a nesting place. It's also a good time to clean out old nesting material from nest boxes that have been used.

Complete any pruning and coppicing work on most deciduous trees and shrubs before the sap begins to rise and before birds are choosing nesting sites. Stack some of the prunings neatly in a corner of the garden or under a hedge to provide a dark, damp hiding place for beetles and centipedes.

Don't worry too much if your pond freezes. Underwater plants can continue to produce oxygen beneath ice, so there's no need to make a hole in the surface. The pond plants need light, though, so if the ice is also covered with snow try to brush it off with a long-handled broom, if you can do so safely. And when the pond is frozen, do make sure to put out some water for the birds each day.

Various kinds of mahonia flower at different times between autumn and late winter, providing nectar for winter-foraging bees and a welcome foretaste of the coming spring.

Remember to go round all your nest boxes and clear out old debris well before the start of the new season.

Index

Page numbers in *italics* refer to entries illustrated in the Plants for wildlife and Wildlife in your garden directories.

Acknowledgements

BBC Books and OutHouse would like to thank the following for their assistance in preparing this book: Phil McCann for advice and guidance; Robin Whitecross for picture research; Lindsey Brown for proofreading; June Wilkins for the index.

Picture credits

Key t = top, b = bottom, l = left, r = right, c = centre

PHOTOGRAPHS
All photographs by Jonathan Buckley except those listed below.

GAP Photos Maxine Adcock 123b; Matt Anker 25; Lee Avison 48t; BBC Magazines Ltd 118b; Pernilla Bergdahl 68cb; Dave Bevan 12, 45t, 46t, 50t, 63b, 64t, 74t, 80, 96cb, 97b, 98br, 100tr; Adrian Bloom 46b, 63t; Richard Bloom 66ct, 76cb; Christina Bollen 114; Mark Bolton 49, 58t & ct; Elke Borkowski 55(2), 57, 63cb, 107; Leigh Clapp 20(1); Claire Davies 79(2); Paul Debois 84ct; David Dixon 79(1); Carole Drake 70t; Heather Edwards 38; Ron Evans 35(1); Geoff du Feu 95ct; FhF Greenmedia 55(1), 58cb, 59ct, 77t, 98bl; Vicki Firmston 33t; Flora Press 72t; Tim Gainey 9t, 98cb; Suzie Gibbons 116l; John Glover 34(2), 34t, 78(1), 78(3), 105; Lucy Griffiths 113; Jerry Harpur 21(1), 34(1), 55(3), 106; Marcus Harpur 29r, 67b; Neil Holmes 54b, 60t, 77ct; Martin Hughes-Jones 73cb, 77bl, 122l; Andrea Jones 104; Lynn Keddie 52b; Geoff Kidd 53t, 79b, 122r; Fiona Lea 78(2), 89br, 99cb, 103(1); Gerald Majumdar 102(2); Zara Napier 55b, 67ct, 98bc, 102(3), 122t; Clive Nichols 9b; Howard Rice 92t, 102(1); JS Sira 76b, 103(2); Jason Smalley 28t; Mel Watson 50b; Jo Whitworth 112; Rob Whitworth 111t; Mark Winwood 47b

iStockphoto Cay-Uwe 52; dumfstar 35(2); HamidEbrahimi 95b; Andrew Howe 81t & b, 82cb, 86ct, 87ct; AlasdairJames 55bl; Viktor_Kitaykin 98t; lauriek 88t; SteveMcBil 91b; merlinpf 118tr; mille19 90ct; NickRH 99ct; Ornitolog82 95cb; prill 100cb; rognar 48b; schnuddel 96b; WebSubstance 99t; WitR 91t

Andrew McIndoe 29l, 40r

Nature Photographers Ltd Dave Bevan 96cb; Frank Blackburn 82b; Hugh Clark 95t; Ron Croucher 92b; Jean Hall 90b; Ernie Janes 93(1); Andrew Merrick 97cb; Owen Newman 94cb; WS Patton 47t; Richard

Revels 23t, 88ct & cb, 101t; Paul Sterry 4, 58b, 63ct, 76t, 77br, 79(3), 82t & ct, 83t, ct, cb & b, 84t, cb & b, 85t, ct, cb & b, 86b, 86t & cb, 87t, cb & b, 89cb, 89br, 90t & ct, 91ct & cb, 93(2), 93t, ct & b, 96t & ct, 97t & ct, 98ct, 99b, 100t, ct & b, 101ct, cb & b, 115t; Roger Tidman 88t, 116t

NHPA Simon Booth 89t; Stephen Dalton 89ct

Sue Gordon 77cb

Marianne Majerus Garden Images Marianne Majerus 2–3
Robin Whitecross 19t, 20(2), 36t, 45b, 51l, 62t, 66b, 73b

ILLUSTRATIONS
Julia Cady 15, 17, 39, 49, 65, 71, 75
Lizzie Harper 31, 35, 37, 38
Janet Tanner 21, 93

Thanks are also due to the following designers and owners, whose gardens appear in the book:

Jill Billington 2–3; Jinny Blom 106; Mark Brown, Leila Cabot Perry Garden, Giverny, France 74b; Beth Chatto, Beth Chatto Gardens, Essex 10; Peter Clay, Herefordshire 26t; Kate Frey, Fetzer Garden, RHS Chelsea Flower Show 2007 21r; Green Farm Plants, Hampshire 70b; Diana Guy, Welcome Thatch, Dorset 18, 26b; Elaine Hughes 103(2); Kevin Hughes, Lymington, Hampshire 109, 110; John Keyes 55(3); Pam Lewis, Sticky Wicket, Dorset 28b, 36b; Christopher Lloyd, Great Dixter, East Sussex 24, 33b, 41, 75; Joy Martin 92t; John Massey, Ashwood Nurseries, Staffordshire 117b; Ulf Nordfjell 34(1); Sarah Raven, Perch Hill, East Sussex 5r; Maureen Sawyer, Southlands, Manchester 111b; June Streets, Horsham, West Sussex 20b; Derry Watkins, Special Plants, Wiltshire 27; Helen Yemm, Eldenhurst, East Sussex 8 and Ketley's, East Sussex 11, 13, 14, 23b, 57, 119, 120b